Shipwreck and Adventures
of Monsieur Pierre Viaud

Engraving from Charles G. T. Garnier, *Voyages Imaginaires, Songes, Visions et Romans Cabalistiques* (Paris, 1787), tome 12, between pages 324 and 325. By permission of the British Library.

Shipwreck and Adventures of Monsieur Pierre Viaud

Translated and Edited by
Robin F. A. Fabel

University of West Florida Press
Pensacola

Library of Congress Cataloging-in-Publication Data

Viaud, Pierre
[Naufrage et aventures de M. Pierre Viaud, natif de
Bordeaux, capitaine de navire. English.]
Shipwreck and adventures of Monsieur Pierre Viaud /
translated and edited by Robin F.A. Fabel.
p. cm.
Translation of: Naufrage et aventures de M. Pierre Viaud,
natif de Bordeaux, capitaine de navire.
Previously attributed to Jean Gaspard Dubois-Fontanelle, the
editor of the French ed.
ISBN 0-8130-1000-4
1. Viaud, Pierre. 2. Survival (after airplane accidents,
shipwrecks, etc.) 3. Shipwrecks—Florida. I. Fabel, Robin F. A.,
1934– . II. Dubois-Fontanelle, Jean Gaspard, 1737–1812.
G530.V48 1990
910.4'5—dc20 90-33552 CIP

The University of West Florida Press is a member of University
Presses of Florida, the scholarly publishing agency of the State
University System of Florida. Books are selected for publication
by faculty editorial committees at each of Florida's nine public
universities: Florida A&M University (Tallahassee), Florida At-
lantic University (Boca Raton), Florida International University
(Miami), Florida State University (Tallahassee), University of
Central Florida (Orlando), University of Florida University of
Florida (Gainesville), University of North Florida (Jacksonville),
University of South Florida (Tampa), University of West Florida
(Pensacola).

Orders for books published by all member presses should be
addressed to University Presses of Florida, 15 NW 15th St.,
Gainesville, FL 32611.

Printed in the United States of America on acid-free paper.

Contents

Acknowledgments

Without considerable help, my wish to produce a new edition and translation of Viaud's *Naufrage* would have remained nothing but an intriguing fantasy.

My first acquaintance with the work was in Elizabeth Griffith's quaint translation on microcard in the microfilm center of Auburn University's library. Its curator, Harmon Stratton, has been unfailingly helpful in finding arcane materials for me.

My subsequent conviction that *Naufrage* was more than an exercise in harrowing fiction came from serendipity. While searching for material on the economy of British West Florida in a castle in Scotland, I happened upon George Swettenham's letter to James Grant describing Viaud's rescue. I am most grateful to Oliver Russell of Ballindalloch Castle, Banffshire, for allowing me access to the Grant Papers.

The wise and critical eye of Dr. Robert Rea of Auburn did much to improve my introduction to this edition of *Naufrage.* James P. Dyehouse of the University of West Florida possesses intimate local knowledge of the area where Viaud claimed to have wandered, and he detected several implausibilities in the Frenchman's tale, which would otherwise have escaped me.

Thanks to Dr. James Servies's encyclopedic command of Floridian bibliography, my attention was drawn to the valuable testimony of Roger Lamb about Viaud's adventures.

I am grateful too to the staffs of various libraries and depositories in Europe: the British Library, London; the Public Record Office, Kew; the Taylorian Institute, Oxford; the Municipal Archives, Bordeaux; the Bibliothèque Nationale, Paris; and the archives of the Department of Charente–

Inférieure at La Rochelle. Similarly courteous and helpful were the staffs of the Louisiana State Archives, Baton Rouge, the Center for Louisiana Studies, Lafayette, and the New York Historical Society.

My research trips to England, France, Scotland, Louisiana, and New York would have been severely hampered had it not been for financial assistance from the Auburn University Humanities Fund and from an Auburn University grant in aid. The work of translation was speeded by Auburn's allowing me a professional improvement leave in the fall of 1987.

Introduction

In 1768, the publication in Bordeaux of the narrative of Pierre Viaud's shipwreck and wanderings in the Florida wilderness created a sensation. It bore the kind of lengthy title common at the time: *Naufrage et Aventures de M. Pierre Viaud, Natif de Bordeaux, Capitaine de Navire, Histoire véritable, vérifiée sur l'Attestation de Mr. Sevettenham, Commandant du Fort St. Marc des Appalaches.* His tale was exotic, lurid—and not altogether plausible. Vainglorious Captain Viaud might have been, but his was a good story. It included calamity at sea, desert islands, hardships, brushes with death, ingenuity, suspense, encounters with Indians, a fight with an alligator, and even, to give the reader a sinister *frisson*, resort to cannibalism. To pique the reader further the aroma (if not the substance) of sex pervaded the latter part of the narrative, which culminated, as all good adventure stories should, with a happy ending. Against all odds the hero and heroine survived their ordeal and went home.

Viaud had left St. Domingue, as Haiti was then called, for New Orleans as a passenger aboard a small merchant vessel, *Le Tigre*, on 2 January 1766. Storms damaged and blew the ship off course in the Gulf of Mexico. It ran aground on a "reef" (which in reality must have been a sandbank) near Dog Island off the coast of Florida. Fifteen survivors made it to Dog Island. Indians found them and removed six of their number to another island, where they robbed them while they slept and marooned them. These six were the captain of *Le Tigre*, his wife and son, together with Viaud, his black slave, and a business partner, Desclau. Captain La Couture and Desclau drowned while paddling a rotten canoe. The other four made a raft to travel to the mainland, but young La Couture was sick and had to be left behind. Four days later, Viaud and the widow, who were starving, killed the slave and ate him. A party of soldiers from St. Mark's Fort at Apalache discovered the pair after another ten days and then rescued young La Couture. Such, in brief summary, were the contents of *Naufrage*.

The work was widely read in France and swiftly became an international bestseller. Second and third editions emerged from Bordeaux in 1770 and 1772, as well as Paris editions in 1770 and 1780. It was published in English translation in London in 1771, 1774, 1780, 1798, 1800, and 1814. For Swiss and Italian readers there were versions from Neuchâtel in 1770 and Florence in 1772. A German translation was available in Leipzig in 1770 and another from Bayer in 1827. There was even a Finnish version published in Upsala. Philadelphia readers were able to buy a locally produced edition in 1774, and another American edition in identical translation was printed in Dover, New Hampshire, in 1799.

Filmgoers of the twentieth century have been consistently fascinated by the themes of disaster at sea and life on a desert island; *Mysterious Island* (1929, 1961), *The Swiss Family Robinson* (1940, 1960), *Lifeboat* (1944), *Titanic* (1953), *The Admirable Crichton* (1957), *A Night to Remember* (1958), *Lord of the Flies* (1963), *Island of the Blue Dolphin* (1964), *Island of the Lost* (1968), and *The Poseidon Adventure* (1972) provide but ten titles from dozens of possible examples. Eighteenth-century readers had similar tastes. The most famous novel in this genre was of course *The True and Surprising Adventures of Robinson Crusoe*, which Daniel Defoe published in 1719. And, just as the success of *The Poseidon Adventure* would inspire production of a less engrossing sequel, *Beyond the Poseidon Adventure* (1979), so too Defoe wrote lame sequels to his masterpiece.

Nothing would equal the success of the original *Robinson Crusoe*, but Defoe had innumerable imitators, especially in France. In 1787 Charles G. T. Garnier edited an anthology of works of this genre. His *Voyages Imaginaires, Songes, Vi-*

sions et Romans Cabalistiques ran to thirty-nine volumes and included Viaud's *Naufrage*. What distinguished Viaud's from the experiences of Crusoe and the rather less well-known Chevalier de Gastines and others, wrote Garnier, was their ability to enlist natural resources for their survival and even comfort. By contrast, nature abandoned Viaud. He found himself on an utterly barren island at a time of the year when even the weather was hostile. He had no clothes, weapons, or instruments to overcome natural hardships.[1]

Garnier exaggerated. Nature was niggardly, but did offer Viaud certain means of survival, although he did not always use them: game, fish, and mollusks were available on the island. It is true that Viaud lacked most of the artifacts that could ameliorate his condition, but he did have clothes, a knife, and a flint. Meager as these possessions might be, they were crucial in averting death.

The authenticity of *Naufrage* would, in time, be much debated but initially was unquestioned. Probably the first notice of the work was in *L'Année Littéraire* for 1769. Its anonymous reviewer had no doubts: "This book is definitely not a novel: it is the narrative of a shipwreck and of a series of misfortunes which lasted eighty-one days. . . . Nothing could be more engrossing than this work. All of the events of which it consists bear a realistic stamp which would be difficult to convey through falsehood."[2]

Another credulous critic, whose review appeared in *Journal Encyclopédique* a year later, seems to have based his trust in Viaud's truthfulness on something more substantial than the nature of the narrative; it was, he wrote, "bolstered with authentic certificates *which we have seen.*"[3] He continued with

1. Charles G. T. Garnier, *Voyages Imaginaires, Songes, Visions et Romans Cabalistiques* (Paris, 1787), 12: 5.
2. *L'Année Littéraire* 7 (1769): 110, 123.
3. Translator's italics.

the information that "M. Viaud is currently in Bordeaux where, after losing both his money and his health in the shipwreck, he is enduring his bad luck with the same staunchness with which he met the misfortunes whose description we have just read."[4] Two months later, however, in March 1770, appeared a cautiously critical verdict, which endorsed the genuineness of some of Viaud's narrative but added the skeptical reservation that "other [of his] adventures . . . although described with total seriousness, do not seem to me equally true to life."[5]

Even if widely disseminated, which is unlikely, this whiff of disbelief did not affect and probably could not have affected the popularity of Viaud's suspenseful story. The bulk of its readers perhaps corresponded to those of today's *National Enquirer*. They were less interested in verifiable fact than in sensation.

Elizabeth Griffith translated *Naufrage* into English in 1771. The Barbara Cartland of her day, she produced in profusion what used to be called novels of wordly intrigue, with titles like *The Gordian Knot* and *The Delicate Distress*. She seems to have translated *Naufrage* hurriedly and verbosely, affecting poetic diction. Where today we would say, "We were glad when day broke," Griffith wrote, "The welcome morn at length arrived."[6] Where we might write, "By luck we found oysters. They made a tasty meal," Griffith's translation was: "The oysters that we happily found, furnished us with a truly delicious repast."[7] In another instance Griffith wrote, "It happily at the same instant occurred to me that I could more effectually supply this exigence by

4. *Journal Encyclopédique* 20, pt. 2 (January 1770): 212, 229.

5. Quoted in Angus Martin, Vivienne G. Mylne, and Richard Frautschi, eds., *Bibliographie du Genre Romanesque Français, 1751–1800* (London: Mansell; Paris: France Expansion, 1977), p. 154.

6. Jean Gaspard Dubois-Fontanelle, ed., and Elizabeth Griffith, trans., *The Surprizing yet Real and True Voyages and Adventures of Monsieur Pierre Viaud, a French Sea Captain* (Philadelphia: Robert Bell, 1774), p. 81.

7. Ibid., p. 17.

setting fire to the reeds," a prolix way of saying "Luckily it then struck me that I could get what we wanted by burning the reeds."[8] A final illustration of Griffith's style: "We had not the good fortune to meet with any manner of aliment during these two days." Even in the eighteenth century, which was more forgiving of verbal ornamentation than our own, "We chanced on nothing to eat on those two days" would have come more naturally.

Leaner prose would have better suited the narrative of a shipwrecked sailor. Even if one may accept that eighteenth-century readers would have found the style less stilted and affected than do twentieth-century Americans and Britons, Griffith took outrageous liberties. She freely admitted in her preface to using "the same freedom with this work as with my former translations, throwing in a few reflections which naturally occurred in some passages of the narrative. This serves to relieve the dulness of the task." The most egregious of her interpolations was a chauvinistic sentence following a few words of gratitude Viaud had written in appreciation of the kindness shown to him after his rescue by three British officers. "They are worthy sons of a free and gallant nation," added Griffith, "and it must ever be a vain attempt in any of their rival powers [which would have included Viaud's native France] to think of combating their fleets and armies, till they have first raised themselves to a level with their liberty and virtue."[9]

Deficient as Griffith's translation was, it proved very popular. Nowadays, surviving copies of Viaud's narrative are comparatively few. The National Union Catalog shows that the total in English in American libraries is forty. They are all in the translation of Elizabeth Griffith. The British Library, London, has a single copy in a different translation of 1814.

8. Ibid., p. 75.
9. Ibid., p. 140.

English critics did not comment on the quality of the Griffith translation, and in general mentioned Viaud favorably. The *London Magazine* summarized his tale as a "heart-rending narrative, which is unquestionably authentic."[10] The *Critical Review* surprisingly and most uncritically described the work as "a distinct and agreeable narrative." Its reviewer was at pains to ridicule skeptics: "The reader will find these adventures sufficiently authenticated to gain the belief of every rational mind. They will only be deemed fabulous by people of limited understanding and superficial reflexions who refuse credit to those facts which happen out of the common and domestic observations, who are ignorant of the complicated history of mankind."[11]

A writer for the *Monthly Review* was more doubtful. He accepted the reality of Viaud's existence and of the shipwreck, but found "notorious improbability" in other parts of the narrative. He scoffed in particular at Viaud's alleged encounter with lions and tigers in the woods of Florida and at the recovery to health of an adolescent after his body had begun to putrefy. The reviewer had initially suspected the authenticity of the certificate allegedly signed by one of Viaud's rescuers and reproduced with his narrative. However, upon investigation the reviewer had discovered that its author, Lieutenant George Swettenham, was alive in the British Isles and was "a man of too much character to countenance an imposition on the public."[12] He therefore concluded, quite correctly, that the certificate was no hoax.

Bernard Romans impugned Viaud's truthfulness more severely. His criticisms have particular weight in that, unlike English and French *littérateurs*, he knew both the country where Viaud's adventures supposedly occurred and one of the men who had rescued the Frenchman. Romans was a Dutch-born American. His book, *A Concise Natural History*

10. *London Magazine* 40 (April 1771): 225.
11. *Critical Review* 31 (1771): 238–39.
12. *Monthly Review* 44 (1771): 421.

of East and West Florida, was penned in the early 1770s and published in America in 1775. It is interesting, in consequence, that in the book Romans referred to islands off Florida as being "well known for the sufferings of Pierre Viaud," since as far as can be determined, the first version of Viaud's adventures published in America did not appear until 1774. It seems likely that Romans had met people acquainted with French copies, perhaps in Louisiana.

Romans could not believe that the castaways were as hungry as Viaud had alleged. "In a place like this," wrote the American, "where plenty of fish, crabs and oysters are to be had . . . for the trouble of digging, their sufferings cannot be great." A second source of disbelief was the alleged capture of a turkey by Viaud's companion in distress, Madame La Couture. So wary of the human presence were these birds, according to Romans, that if La Couture had caught one, "certainly she must have been a more expert huntress than I ever heard of before." To ascertain the truth of this matter, Romans sought out one of the rescue party who had been present when Madame La Couture appeared with the turkey. He was John Simpson, a trader and Indian interpreter. Simpson told Romans that La Couture had brought to the camp, not a turkey, but a king crab. From this information Romans concocted an implausible hypothesis. The king crab looked a little like a turtle. Taking it for such, Viaud, in writing up the scene, used the French word for turtle, *tortue.* A typesetter then misread the handwritten word "turtle" in the English translation as "turkey."[13] Romans also suspected that a mistranslation of *outarde* resulted in the solecism of bustards, exclusively European birds, in Florida. He was the first commentator to scold Elizabeth Griffith for the quality of her translation.[14]

13. Romans was wrong. Viaud unmistakably meant "turkey." He used the words *la poule d'Inde.*

14. Rembert W. Patrick, introduction to Captain Bernard Romans, *A Concise Natural History of East and West Florida* (New York, 1775; Gainesville: University of Florida Press, 1962), pp. 300–301.

Popular in Britain, *Naufrage* continued to be read as widely in France. In 1787 it was included in the twelfth volume of Garnier's previously mentioned anthology. Doubting neither Viaud's existence nor that his adventures actually took place, Garnier thought it necessary to justify the inclusion of *Naufrage* in a collection of fiction. He noted first that the aims of his anthology were to amuse, to teach, and to interest. *Naufrage* was unquestionably interesting but of more importance, thought Garnier, was the depiction of Viaud's frightful situation and the stages in which, little by little, he was drawn to the very pit of hopelessness. Garnier was surely making oblique reference to the progression of despair that had made Viaud accept murder and cannibalism as the only means of survival.

For twentieth-century readers this crime of Viaud's is probably central, the most memorable event in the narrative. It may not have been so in the 1770s. Not one of the reviewers cited above mentioned it. However, it was probably not so much that readers were unmoved by the incident as that reviewers were unprepared to violate polite convention by discussing barbarity in print. An analogy might be made to the eighteenth-century dramatic convention of not staging violent acts. They often occurred as vital elements in plays, but were contrived to take place offstage.

This explanation will not suffice to explain Romans's failure to mention the murder. He was not part of the world of letters. A literate New World engineer rather than an Old World critic, he was not the man to be hobbled by polite bookish manners.[15] The explanation for his silence must be sought elsewhere and perhaps lies in his contempt for blacks. Although he was prepared to admit that they were "a useful part of creation" and deplored unnecessary cru-

---

15. Romans was born in the Netherlands about 1720. Educated in Britain, from 1757 he was in North America, first as a surveyor in the southern colonies; then as a botanist; then as a fortress engineer and finally an artillery officer for the American revolutionaries. He died in 1784.

elty to them, he also generalized that "Treachery, theft, stubbornness and idleness . . . these qualities are natural to them."[16] If a choice had to be made, Romans most likely would have considered a black person more expendable than a white. In short it seems that he would have seen no reason to quarrel with Viaud's desperate justification that his slave's *raison d'être* was, whether by living or dying, to serve his owner.

By 1780 there may have occurred a change in sentiment about the propriety of mentioning barbarous behavior. In his introduction to *Naufrage,* Garnier quoted at length an addition to the preface of the 1780 edition (which is otherwise identical to the 1770 and 1772 Editor's Note reproduced in this volume). It squarely addressed murder and cannibalism. Its author, who is generally thought to be Jean G. Dubois-Fontanelle, wrote that some readers of the early editions had been revolted by Viaud's killing and eating his servant. He attempted no justification but begged readers to consider the circumstances. His own view was that the combination of starvation and despair might not justify but might explain Viaud's actions. Some readers, he continued, because they refused to believe that such a crime could have occurred, insisted on regarding *Naufrage* as nothing but a novel. To counter this skepticism, the author of the preface vaguely cited "an infinity of examples" of cannibalism among sea travelers and, more precisely, the case of a ship's crew who ran out of provisions and resorted to cannibalism on a voyage from New York to the Canary Islands in the same month that Viaud made his ill-fated trip aboard *Le Tigre.*[17] The facts of this incident, which concerned the sloop *Peggy,* were well attested and widely reported in the press.[18]

16. Romans, *Concise History,* p. 105.
17. Garnier, *Voyages Imaginaires,* 12: 215, 223.
18. The tale was related in *London Magazine* 35 (1766): 315–18; *Scots Magazine* 28 (1766): 352–57; and, more fully, in David Harrison, *The Deliv-*

With the passing of the years, doubts about Viaud's veracity grew. *Naufrage* appeared again during the French
Revolution in a collection of novels in a section titled "Romans Merveilleux." The editors justified its inclusion with
the following logic: "The voyage of M. Viaud is either true
or made up. If it is fiction, it belongs here. If it is true, it
has the appearance of fiction" and thus still merited a
place.[19]

So, in successive decades, *Naufrage* appeared in antholo-
gies of imaginary voyages. The publication in 1811 of memoirs asserting the reality of Viaud's voyage and adventures
did little to dent growing skepticism. When their author,
Roger Lamb, had joined the Ninth Infantry Regiment of the
British army in 1773, among its members were two serving
officers who had been among Viaud's rescuers in 1776. One
of them, Lieutenant George Swettenham (whom Lamb calls
Sweetman) frequently reminisced about his encounter with
Viaud; the other, James Wright, would describe in repug-
nant detail the scraps of decaying human flesh that Viaud
and his companion carried with them when he discovered
them. Of *Naufrage* Lamb concluded that "however extraordinary this narrative may be, I have no reason to doubt
of its veracity."[20] A further layer of doubt was added in 1828
when *Naufrage* was alleged to be no more than a reprint

erance of *Captain David Harrison of the Sloop Peggy of New York on the Voyage
from Fyal, one of the Western Isles to New York* (London: n.p., 1766). French
readers half a century later would have been readier to believe in Viaud's
swift descent to savagery. The tale of the wreck of the frigate *Medusa* was
Viaud's story writ large. When *Medusa* foundered, 150 men and women
sought safety on a raft made from timbers. Fifteen survivors gave evidence
that, desperate with hunger, the castaways had, within days, resorted to
fighting, murder, and cannibalism. To lighten the raft, wounded men and
women were thrown overboard while still alive. See Alexander McKee,
Death Raft (New York: Scribner's, 1975).

19. *Nouvelle Bibliothèque Universelle des Romans* (Paris: Maradan et alia,
1798), vol. 1, pt. 2, p. 47.

20. Roger Lamb, *Memoir of his own Life* (Dublin: Jones, 1811), pp. 61,
75, 85, 87.

of Dubois-Fontanelle's 1768 novel *Les Effets des Passions, ou Mémoires de M. Floricourt*.[21] Over a century later, in 1936, this canard was reproduced in the standard twenty-nine-volume *Bibliotheca Americana*. The incidents in *Naufrage* were unequivocally labeled "imaginary." In fact *Les Effets des Passions*, although packed with action, bears no other resemblance to *Naufrage*. It contains no shipwreck, no Florida, no Viaud and, if it is stylistically typical of Dubois-Fontanelle, he did not pen the simpler, more concrete prose of *Naufrage*. With justice, for it is a very bad novel, few copies of *Les Effets des Passions* now exist, although a copy may still be found in the Bibliothèque Nationale in Paris. The false identification of *Naufrage* with *Les Effets des Passions* in 1936 is the more surprising because the libel had been scotched twenty years previously by the French author of an academic thesis on the literary influence of *Robinson Crusoe*.[22]

Whether believed to be fact or fiction, Viaud's shocking story continued to fascinate the masses in the twentieth century. A weak retelling of his trials appeared in a French pulp magazine in 1932,[23] and a commercial press in London found it worthwhile to reproduce a restatement of the narrative by Thomas Washington Metcalfe in 1935. It is a paraphrase with some pointless but no significant additions.[24] What is interesting about Metcalfe's version of the story is that, watered down though it was, it sufficed to convert an intelligent anonymous reviewer for the *Times Literary*

21. Cited in Joseph Sabin, Wilberforce Eames and R. W. G. Vail, eds., *Bibliotheca Americana: A Dictionary of Books Relating to America* (New York: Bibliographical Society of America, 1868– 1936), 26: 492.

22. William E. Mann, *Robinson Crusoe en France* (Paris: Université de Paris, Faculté des Lettres, 1916), p. 137n.

23. T. Dorsenne, *"L'Homme qui Mangea un Négre,"* Lectures pour Tous (Paris: Librairie Hachette, 1932).

24. Thomas Washington Metcalfe, *Captain Viaud and Madame La Couture: Their true and surprising Adventures, Shipwreck and Distresses: A Narrative mainly transcribed from the Letters of Captain Viaud* (London: Nicholson and Watson, 1935).

Supplement from disbelief to acceptance. "It is difficult to exaggerate the scepticism which sophisticated readers will bring to the first pages of this 'true' narrative," he began. He concluded, however, that long before the story is fully told "we believe that Captain Viaud is telling the truth about his ordeal as far as his sufferings allow him to recall it."[25]

The *TLS* reviewer, evidently no historian, believed in the authenticity of *Naufrage* from internal evidence. He found its characters plausible and the enormity of their crime consistent with their nature and circumstances. The description of their sufferings he judged "as vivid as it is convincing." Mark F. Boyd, who *was* a historian, reinforced this assertion of belief in the following year, 1936.[26] In 1943 Charles L. Mowat based a similar endorsement on limited but valid documentary evidence in his *East Florida as a British Province, 1763–1784.*[27]

Unfortunately for the dissemination of truth, the *Bibliotheca Americana* was probably much more widely consulted than Boyd's state journal article or Mowat's monograph, especially as neither author accorded Viaud more than passing reference. More than thirty years later, Philip Gove gave learned consideration to the authenticity of *Naufrage* and accurately observed that no satisfactory study of the work had yet clarified its uncertain status.[28] Gove suspended judgment on the matter but, in omitting it from his list of imaginary voyages, showed an inclination to believe.

What commentators have not done, in spite of a general tendency to extend limited credulity, is to look for contem-

25. *Times Literary Supplement,* 10 October 1935, p. 625.

26. Mark F. Boyd, "The Fortifications at San Marcos de Apalache (St. Mark's, Wakulla Co., Florida)," *Florida Historical Quarterly* 15 (1936).

27. Charles L. Mowat, *East Florida as a British Province, 1763–1784* (Berkeley: University of California Press, 1943), p. 179.

28. Philip Babcock Gove, *The Imaginary Voyage in Prose Fiction* (New York: Octagon Press, 1975), p. 41n81.

porary verification of Viaud's tall tale. The exception was Charles Mowat, who found important confirmation in the correspondence of the governor of East Florida but who, perhaps from lack of interest, took his researches on Viaud no further.

Discovery of confirmatory contemporary manuscripts would do much to diminish the doubt surrounding Viaud's novelistic narrative. It is true that part of it is, and always will be, impossible to verify. During the period when he and Madame La Couture and a slave wandered in the wilderness of the Florida mainland, they met nobody, the slave died in the process, and Madame La Couture left no memoirs of their ordeal. For that section of the story the reader has no evidence except Viaud's words. That period lasted a mere two weeks. Viaud had much to say about himself in the times that preceded and succeeded that fortnight. If what he wrote about these periods could be substantiated, the plausibility of his claims about a time when facts cannot be verified would be enhanced, although this two-week period remains the most dubious part of *Naufrage*. Viaud was then at his lowest ebb physically and mentally: his recollections of what happened would inevitably have been cloudy, and it was here that his collaborator, Dubois-Fontanelle, is most likely to have added fictional embellishments.

Actually, relevant unpublished and hitherto unnoticed manuscripts exist in France, Scotland, and England. They confirm more than they disprove Viaud's story. Of prime importance are materials in the provincial Archives de la Charente-Inférieure at La Rochelle which reveal that Viaud truly existed and that he was what he, if not his editor, claimed himself to be. He was born, not in Bordeaux, as the title page of *Naufrage* alleged, but in St. Nazaire on the west coast of France on 16 September 1725, the son of Etienne Viaud and Marie Ranfonneau. He was earning a living at sea by the age of sixteen.

His first two recorded voyages were aboard the royal vessels *Profonde* and *Gironde*, in which he occupied the lowly positions of cabin boy and apprentice cabin boy respectively. At eighteen, on *Ajée*, he was away from home for more than twelve months. Less than a year later, in 1746, he embarked on another long voyage aboard *Alcion*. Surviving records do not reveal what countries he visited but, on the ship *L'Hirondelle* in 1750, he visited Cap François in what is now Haiti. Probably *L'Hirondelle* was a merchant vessel, but his next voyage, in 1751, was a cruise of three months on the king's ship *Zéphir*, with the rank of sublieutenant.

In 1754 he journeyed to the west coast of Africa as a gunner aboard the ship *Langeronne*. In the following year he went in *La Marguerite*, a *grelette* (evidently a smaller vessel), on another voyage to Cap François. For the first time, as far as the record shows, he was in command, and was suitably rewarded with pay at ten times the rate he had earned as a mere gunner or sublieutenant. In 1760, he received a passport from the French consul at the Spanish port of Vigo. He had arrived there from Martinique as second in command of the ship *La Marie*, which was decommissioned in Spain.

In 1761, when he was thirty-six, Viaud wrote to the lieutenant general in charge of the Royal Office of Admiralty at Marennes. He wanted to take the usual examination for obtaining a certificate as a ship's captain in the merchant marine, and alleged, in support of his suitability, that he had acquired a perfect knowledge of the navigation, maneuver, and the running of ships through experience on long cruises in both peacetime and war. He received his certificate on 2 October 1761.[29] In France there was less distinction between officers in the royal and merchant services than in other nations.

A nineteenth-century American, whose family had a close acquaintance with Viaud, attested that even though

29. Archives de la Charente-Inférieure, La Rochelle, Series B, no. 144, fols. 1-11.

he was merely an officer in the merchant marine, Viaud occupied a much higher relative position than a similar person would have done in America, since French mariners of every rank were registered and liable to naval duties in case of need. That he engaged in commerce was no reason for assuming that he did not belong to the king's navy, since naval officers could and did command merchant vessels.[30] Viaud described himself as *capitaine de navire* (signifying merchant navy captain), coupled with the words *officier bleu*. These last, meaning literally "blue officer," baffled Elizabeth Griffith, who (perhaps associating them with "the Blues," the British royal household cavalry) thought that Viaud was claiming to be an army as well as a naval officer. In fact *officier bleu* was a naval term for which our usage, "naval reserve officer," would be the closest equivalent.[31]

The Seven Years' War ended in 1763 and a great many naval officers found themselves out of work. Perhaps Viaud was one of them, but by February 1765, according to his narrative, he was commanding the merchantman *L'Aimable Suzette*, bound from Bordeaux for St. Domingue. No record of this specific voyage has survived, but there is evidence in the Bordeaux Municipal Archives that there was a merchant vessel of that name registered in Bordeaux at the time, which sailed to the West Indies.[32] If it was, as seems sure, the vessel referred to by Viaud, his post was on a sizable vessel with a crew of twenty-six.

Britain has two documentary collections containing unpublished manuscripts which support the validity of the latter part of Viaud's narrative. One is the East Florida correspondence in the Public Record Office at Kew, part of which

30. Thomas Watts De Peyster, *De Peyster and Watts Genealogical Reference* (New York: Tivoli, 1854), p. 191.

31. William Falconer, *An Universal Dictionary of the Marine* (London, 1780; reprint, New York: Augustus M. Kelley, 1970), p. 339.

32. Archives Municipales de Bordeaux, Fonds Depit, fol. 142.

was used by Charles Mowat in his comments on Viaud. The other is the James Grant Papers, Ballindalloch Castle, Scotland, which have been quite ignored as far as they relate to Viaud.

As East Florida's governor, Grant had naturally reported unusual happenings in his province, especially if they concerned foreigners, to his superiors in London. Among other items in a long letter of 5 August 1766 to the Board of Trade, he summarized Viaud's account of his adventures after arrival in St. Domingue. Though much shorter, it accorded closely with the contents of *Naufrage*, which was, therefore, neither invented by, nor to please, Dubois-Fontanelle: Viaud had yet to meet him. The single major omission from this early account is the cannibalism episode but, as I shall show, there is evidence for that crime from one who talked with Viaud even before Grant did.

The governor's letter provided additional information confirming parts of Viaud's narrative. It derived from a Creek chief, Talachea, who was concerned to avoid trouble with the British authorities. Talachea confessed to Grant that young warriors of his nation, while out hunting, had happened on and killed a party of shipwrecked Frenchmen. They were murders of revenge: the French had killed two women and a boy of their tribe. Grant was skeptical of this justification and spoke sternly to Talachea's messenger, but it accords exactly with Viaud's version of what happened.

The governor commented on Viaud's poor physical condition and said that he had taken good care of him and, just as Viaud alleged in *Naufrage*, had paid for his voyage to New York and given him pocket money. Grant also confirmed that Madame La Couture and her son departed St. Mark's for New Orleans, with the additional detail that they intended to go by way of Pensacola, at the time the capital of British West Florida. That the records of that colony make no mention of their arrival does not falsify Grant's assertion, since no comprehensive list of ship arrivals in West Florida for that period has survived, or perhaps ever existed. The governor also supplied the information that the La Coutures were followed to New Orleans by three other shipwrecked Frenchmen. Indians had captured them and then given them up to the British at the insistence of the officer commanding St. Mark's Fort, George Swettenham. This information was unknown to Viaud, who was fully persuaded that all his shipmates were dead (p. 119). The discrepancy may be explained by the interval between Viaud's leaving St. Augustine on 21 July and Grant's writing his report on 5 August. Grant could have learned of the survival of the three Frenchmen during the intervening fifteen days.[33]

Viaud was properly grateful for Grant's generosity (p. 121). The provincial contingency fund paid for most of the expenses incurred in setting the Frenchman on his feet again: two guineas for clothing, forty-three shillings to a Mr. Cumings for provisions for Viaud's sea voyage, and thirty-six shillings for his passage to New York. In *Naufrage* Viaud wrote that the passage cost thirty-seven shillings, a sum so close to the actual cost as to enhance rather than diminish his credibility (p. 121). Viaud may therefore be believed when he notes, in the same paragraph, that upon his departure Governor Grant pressed ten guineas upon him. It was a substantial gesture, for Grant did not charge it to the contingency fund. For purposes of comparison, it may be noted that a corporal in the British army at the time would not have earned ten guineas at the standard rate of pay in six months.

Of perhaps more importance than Grant's official correspondence are the informal letters of the commandant of Fort St. Mark, George Yort Swettenham, an Irish lieutenant of the Ninth Infantry Regiment. Viaud acknowledged that

33. James Grant to the Board of Trade, 5 August 1766, Public Record Office, CO 5/548: 199–207. I am most grateful to Oliver Russell of Ballindalloch Castle, Banffshire, Scotland, for permission to use and quote from the James Grant Papers.

he owed his life to two men. One was Ensign James Wright, who found him on a Florida beach when he was on the point of death. The other was Swettenham, who had sent Wright to the beach.

Swettenham had received news of a shipwreck from James Burgess, a trader at one of the Lower Creek villages near Apalache.[34] This intelligence reinforced a report from an Indian that he had chanced on a white corpse among the jetsam on a local beach. Swettenham responded with enterprise and persistence. He dispatched Wright in a canoe to investigate. Appalling weather hindered the ensign's search and, having found nothing, he returned. Swettenham made him go back in a larger boat with a number of men. As a consequence they found Viaud and Madame La Couture "in the most miserable condition."[35]

Neither Wright nor Swettenham were figments of a novelist's imagination. They both figure in the annual lists of British army officers published at the time. In one sense it is unfortunate that Ensign Wright, who actually found the French couple, and who, according to Naufrage, tried to eat the dried flesh of Viaud's poor slain servant, apparently left no memoir of his adventures in Florida. Given a choice, however, it was better that Swettenham recorded his experience, because we know from his letters that the certificate appearing above his name in every edition of Naufrage was authentic. "I have given a certificate at his [Viaud's] request," wrote Swettenham to his friend, James Grant, "and have directed him to wait on you with it."

Wright found Viaud on 6 May. They arrived at St. Mark's on 8 May. Only six days later, on 14 May, Swettenham wrote about Viaud to the governor. The Frenchman had not hesitated to confess to cannibalism, and Swettenham wrote graphically about it while Viaud was at hand and

34. Burgess to Swettenham, 5 May 1766, Bundle 243, Grant Papers, Ballindalloch Castle, Banffshire, Scotland.
35. Swettenham to Grant, 14 May 1766, ibid.

when his words would still be fresh in the lieutenant's ears: "They were obliged to kill a negro for their subsistence, the story of which is shocking—his tying the hands, his handkerchief over his eyes, his sharping [*sic*] his knife and then cutting his throat—is terrible. A few scraps of this miserable wretch was their provision when Mr. Wright took them up."

It is satisfying to the scholarly sense to have this confirmation of the most sensational segment of *Naufrage*, over which almost every other contemporary commentator passed in silence, especially as it makes clear, in a way that Swettenham's certificate did not fully clarify, that the motive for the murder was cannibalism. Somehow it is even more satisfactory that the lieutenant did not treat the episode with insouciance. He was shocked, horrified. At the same time he did not find it unforgivable. He believed that "this poor man . . . is now really an object of compassion." He also thought Viaud a gentleman, and one cannot but suspect that Swettenham would not have condoned his crime, had Viaud not belonged to the same social class as himself. Even when killing was concerned, Britons of the 1760s did not apply the same penalties to all classes alike—as, to take but one example, their attitudes to dueling attest.

One of the most incredible incidents in *Naufrage* was the survival for nineteen days of a desperately sick teenager, alone on a desert island, sustained by nothing but a pile of oysters and some water-filled shells. This feat excited the scornful derision of a London reviewer and, no doubt, other readers. Swettenham confirmed its truth. When found, young La Couture, just as Viaud would relate, could not walk, could scarcely speak, and, in Swettenham's opinion, could not have lived for another twelve hours.

An anonymous reviewer of his book in the *Providence Gazette*, 16 July 1774, wrote that Viaud "in the fall of 1766, was for some months entertained at the house of Mr. Depeyster, merchant, in New York, and was well known and respected by many of its genteelest inhabitants during his stay, from whence he sailed to Old France in the spring of 1767." If true, one might expect to find contemporary references to the Frenchman in the New York newspapers and in the correspondence of the New York establishment. As far as I can discover, there are none. I suspect that the Providence reviewer added a bit of guesswork to Viaud's account: Viaud wrote nothing in *Naufrage* about socializing with the gentry of New York. The probability is that he spent several weeks recovering from the physical effects of his ordeal and was not active in society.

There *is* confirmation of his sailing to and arrival in New York and of his receiving extended hospitality from the De Peyster family. The East Florida contingency account listed, as noted here, that thirty-six shillings were spent on Viaud's passage to New York. They were paid to a "Captain Osburn."[36] The *New York Mercury* of 11 August 1766 reported that in the previous week the sloop *Manby* had arrived in New York from St. Augustine under the command of a Captain John Osborne, surely the same man. The date given by Viaud in *Naufrage* for his arrival in New York was 3 August (p. 122).

The De Peysters were a New York family of Belgian origin who had settled in America in the 1640s and subsequently prospered. The most eminent of them in the 1760s was Abraham De Peyster, treasurer of the province of New York. Viaud's benefactor was James, one of Abraham's several sons. James, born in 1726, held a militia commission and was unpopular or unlucky during the Stamp Act riots, when his beautiful mansion, Ranelagh, was sacked by the mob.[37] Despite his military affiliation, De Peyster's life was devoted to commerce. He had an interest in one hundred vessels and enjoyed a reputation as the most benevolent man in New York.[38]

36. PRO, CO 5/548:397.
37. De Peyster, *De Peyster and Watts*, p. 28.
38. Walter W. Spooner, *Historical Families of America* (New York: New York Families' Publishing Association, 1907), 1: 4, 9, 19.

Other than the surprising swiftness of his passage, there is little reason, therefore, to question Viaud's assertions that he stayed with De Peyster for six months and that on 6 February 1767, he captained a small vessel across the Atlantic for his benefactor, arriving in Nantes on 27 February. Such incidents do not excite incredulity in the same way as bear chases and alligator fights.

In view of the close bond of friendship that Viaud allegedly had formed with Madame La Couture, it would have been natural for her and Viaud to exchange letters. If so, none has come to light. She may have been illiterate: marriage to a sea captain by no means implied education in the eighteenth century. This is a guess, and Madame La Couture remains a mysterious figure. We do not even know her Christian name, let alone anything of her subsequent career in Louisiana, assuming she arrived there. Research in Louisiana archives has revealed only one minute item which might, or might not, indicate what happened to her. Twenty years after the wreck of Le Tigre, on the second German Coast of Louisiana, about forty miles above New Orleans, François André sold a small farm to one Jacques Estaire. It was described as bounded below by the Widow La Couture's.[39] For Madame La Couture's son, there has survived not even one clue to his destiny.

Viaud was evidently a one-book author. He features in no dictionaries of French literature. Information about *Naufrage* has to be sought under the name of Jean Gaspard Dubois-Fontanelle. Viaud may have died soon after the publication of *Naufrage*. Although a reviewer in 1769 insisted that his health had been restored,[40] we know from his narrative that he had suffered from a prolonged

39. Glenn Conrad, *Saint Jean-Baptiste des Allemands: Abstracts of the Civil Records of St. John the Baptist Parish with Genealogy and Index, 1753–1803* (Lafayette: Center for Louisiana Studies, University of Southwest Louisiana, 1981), p. 104.

40. *L'Année Littéraire* 7 (1769): 123.

illness even before his trials aboard *Le Tigre* and in Florida. We also know that, subjected to similar ordeals, Madame La Couture showed superior stamina. It is possible that Viaud suffered from a weak constitution and died shortly after the first publication of his book: we cannot tell.

Yet we can tell much otherwise about Viaud from *Naufrage*, not all of it to his credit. An essential question is not so much whether he strayed from the precise truth as how big a liar was he? For there can be no doubt that *Naufrage* is much more than the unvarnished truth. Research has confirmed the existence of Viaud, Swettenham, Wright, and De Peyster, among others mentioned in the narrative. There is documentary evidence too for the shipwreck, cannibalism, and rescue. But there is much else between the wreck and the rescue which cannot be verified, and a great deal of it is so illogical, inconsistent, and contrary to normal human experience as to excite profound skepticism. Common sense suggests that the central portion of *Naufrage* has been fictionalized: novelistic flesh applied to factual bones. If so, a reason is easy to find. Details are undiscoverable, but it is evident that Viaud collaborated with Dubois-Fontanelle, a prolific French novelist almost certainly more interested in sales than in accuracy.

The least plausible incidents in *Naufrage* all occur on the mainland. The bear chasing Viaud's servant up a tree, the wild beasts ringing the campfire, Viaud's killing a twelve-foot alligator with a pointed stick—all have the flavor of a boys' adventure story, a touch of Indiana Jones. It is entirely possible that they were all inventions of Dubois-Fontanelle, designed to spice what would otherwise be a depressing and unsalable record of privation. The evidence for the mainland episode is mixed. Although Governor Grant accepted that Viaud and Madame La Couture had wandered on the mainland for a fortnight,[41] George Swetten-

41. Grant to the Board of Trade, 5 August 1766, PRO, CO 5/548:207.

ham reported that Ensign Wright had found the castaways, not on the mainland, but "on the island about thirty or forty miles from this place [i.e., St. Mark's Fort, Apalache] and six miles distant from the shore."[42]

An instance where one may suspect that Dubois-Fontanelle rewrote Viaud's bald narrative in the interests of drama at the expense of consistency and accuracy may be found early in *Naufrage* (p. 45). Perhaps a Dutch sailor did indeed drown while trying to swim to shore from the wreck of *Le Tigre,* an entirely believable, sad, but rather tame episode. In *Naufrage* the sailor preceded his swim with a literary speech (to evoke pity), and after touching but not achieving his goal (suspense), was dashed to death against a rock (tragic waste). But there are no rocks in St. George Sound (factually false), and probably there never were, for elsewhere in the narrative, seek as he would, Viaud could not find so much as a pebble in the area (inconsistency).

Another source of error is the unavoidable haziness of the survivor's recollection of a prolonged ordeal two years after the event. Again one example may make the point. By his own account, Viaud was on the point of death when he was rescued and certainly he must have been utterly exhausted. So when Madame La Couture arrived with food on that day, he remembered it as wild turkey. One of the rescue party, John Simpson, who was presumably in good mental and physical health, recalled her find as a king crab when he talked about the incident with Bernard Romans. That the lady found a crab is much easier to believe, but the discrepancy does not mean that Madame La Couture did not successfully forage for the substance of a meal. In short, the error in factual detail is not extremely important.

Some of the most preposterous adventures of Viaud concern wild animals, whether lions, tigers, bears, or alligators. These encounters were probably fictional, but some com-

42. Swettenham to Grant, 14 May 1766, Bundle 243, Grant Papers.

ment on them is appropriate. They were more possible than twentieth-century or even eighteenth-century European readers are or were aware. So great was the ridicule evidently evoked by these parts of his narrative that, from 1780, references to lions and tigers disappear from French versions of *Naufrage,* though not from the numerously reproduced English editions in the Griffith translation. The editor of these later French versions amended the words on p. 85 to read: "In our ever-growing terror, we thought we saw among the creatures surrounding us animals of the fiercest species, even of kinds which did not exist in the region." Perhaps Viaud approved this change. It is also possible that he did not—that he was dead by 1780, and when he had referred to tigers and lions, he meant what he wrote. Such words were used in the southern parts of eighteenth-century America to describe beasts unlike the huge carnivores of Africa and India. Refugees fleeing through Georgia in 1781 saw mountain lions. Like Viaud, they also met bears and, again like Viaud, caulked an old pirogue with cloth from their belongings.[43]

That Viaud's little group should encounter a bear is unexceptionable. The contemporary naturalist William Bartram wrote that bears were very common in the Florida region, although he had been unable to confirm that they attacked humans.[44] Identifying Viaud's tigers is more troublesome. Both the French *tigre* and its English equivalent, then often spelled "tyger," were used in the eighteenth century for a variety of American animals, including cougars and jaguars. It may be noted that in an official list of imports to Britain from Florida in 1774 were listed eight "tyger" skins

43. Timothy Dwight, *Travels in New England and New York* (New York, 1823; reprint, Cambridge, Mass.: Belknap Press of Harvard University Press, 1967), 1: 226–27.

44. William Bartram, *Travels of William Bartram,* ed. Mark Van Doren (New York: Dover Publications Inc., 1955), p. 232.

as well as lion skins.[45] The probability, however, is that in his terror Viaud misidentified the animals.

An incident in *Naufrage* that stretches to the limit the credulity of the twentieth-century reader is Viaud's fighting, conquering, and killing a large alligator with no weapon but a pointed stick. Bartram described a contest he observed in Florida with an alligator of similar length to Viaud's, twelve feet. "[The attackers] formed javelins of saplings, pointed and hardened with fire; these they thrust down his throat into his bowels, which caused the monster to bellow and roar hideously; but his strength and fury were so great that he easily wrenched and twisted them out of their hands and . . . kept his enemies at a distance."[46] Since his method of attack was clearly practiced by others, Viaud's story is, however implausible, just possible, particularly if, as fishermen are prone to do, he exaggerated the length of his adversary.

These minor modifications to incredulity about exotic beasts do not, of course, make *Naufrage* a ship's log. It is not comprehensive and is, in many places, maddeningly imprecise. For a mariner skilled in navigation, Viaud was astonishingly vague in describing his various moves. In his wandering among the islands off the Florida coast, he never indicated what the sun's position would have shown, even to a landsman: whether he and his companions were traveling eastward or westward. The islands visited by Viaud seem to have stretched in a chain, running roughly northeast to southwest. Dog Island, on which he was wrecked, was at one end, the most northerly of the chain. The others now form St. George Island, which is very long and extremely narrow in places. In the late eighteenth century it was not one island but at least four islets.[47]

45. T64/276, Great Britain, Public Record Office, Kew.
46. Bartram, *Travels,* p. 210.
47. See Bernard Romans's map, "Part of the Province of East Florida,"

From Dog Island all the castaways were taken to an island about nine miles away, on which the Indian, Antonio,
had a hut (pp. 55–56). From there Viaud, Desclau, the two
La Coutures, and the servant were taken to four more islands on which, wrote Viaud in his note H, he was set
down. Antonio then marooned the party of five on another
island (p. 59), the second of the four, from which they
waded across to yet another of them, the third of the four,
in search of food and water, such as they had already found
there (p. 61). From this island, three of the party reached
the last of the four islands previously visited, again by wading, where they recovered a pirogue (p. 65). If, as seems
sure, this fourth island was adjacent to Antonio's island (p.
68), then the general pattern for the marooned castaways
was to work their way southwest to northeast. Including
Dog Island, Antonio's island, the island on which they were
marooned, the two islands to which they waded, and one
other on which Antonio set them down, Viaud spent time
on a total of six islands.

Viaud was not merely vague, he was also incompetent.
As Romans indicated, there was food to be found by those
with ingenuity. In September 1763, when Richard Savery's
schooner, *Dublin*, was lost on the Bahama Bank, the castaways had survived on rats, whelks, cormorants, and palmetto cabbages.[48] Viaud seems, by contrast, to have been
singularly unenterprising in foraging for food. If he truly
was on the mainland in April, he should have been able
to find blueberries in abundance.[49] And, once deprived of
firearms, he never seems to have tried other means of catch-
ing seabirds, which, like palmetto, abound in the region.

---

drawn in 1772. It can be found in John P. Ware, introduction to P. Lee
Phillips, *Notes on the Life and Works of Bernard Romans* (Deland, Fla., 1924;
reprint, Gainesville: University of Florida Press, 1975).

48. *South Carolina Gazette*, 10 December 1763.

49. I am grateful for this information to James P. Dyehouse of the University of West Florida.

Other than the lucky finds of a roebuck, rattlesnakes, and turtles, the castaways' main sustenance came from the seashore. Unless the move was entirely fictional, it was an almost fatal error of judgment for Viaud to veer away from the coast (p. 90).

He showed that he could successfully build rafts with the most meager supplies and implements—in one instance, a raft good enough to cross a six-mile stretch of sea with two people aboard (p. 83). (It is hard to understand, incidentally, why Viaud was content to glide over this twelve-hour ordeal in one sentence.) His ability at raft construction is undoubted. What is questionable is a different kind of competence. Why did he not resort to this very obvious expedient—one which came to mind as soon as *Le Tigre* struck the reef near Dog Island (p. 43) — much sooner, when there would have been more suitable materials available and more hands to use them?

More important than faulty memory, and as important in distorting his narrative, is Viaud's vanity. He was a blatant boaster. He described decisions as mistakes only if other people made them. He consistently praised himself lavishly. On its own, the background music of self-congratulation pervading his tale would render implicit belief in *Naufrage* as an accurate chronicle quite impossible. Castigating the dead Captain La Couture, Viaud claimed for himself all credit for the decisions that saved *Le Tigre* from shipwreck prior to arrival near Florida (pp. 40–42). Nearly all the other castaways were cowards: only Viaud kept his courage throughout (p. 43). Refitting the pirogue, a bad idea, was conceived by others (p. 65); looking for the gun-flint, a life-saving idea (p. 66), was Viaud's. The others mocked when he accurately declared the pirogue unseaworthy (p. 71), but Viaud alone thought of building the raft that took the castaways to the mainland (p. 73). It was Viaud, not Madame La Couture, who had the good if belated inspiration of clearing their path by firing the landscape (p. 96); it was Viaud who revived her son when he first fell sick (p. 77), and it was he, not she, who saved the boy's life by insisting on returning to the island where he had been stranded (p. 113).

Portraying himself as a paragon did not quite work. Viaud had clearly determined to jettison the teenaged La Couture when he became seriously sick, and to let him die alone on a desert island. The lad's alleged demand that he be abandoned (which Viaud has him express, incidentally, in uncommonly fine diction for a boy of fifteen) does not conceal the callousness of the deed. Moreover, Viaud suggested that his intention to kill his servant was unformed until Madame La Couture silently but unmistakably urged him to it. She then held the slave, according to his account, while he administered the lethal blows. This finely detailed implication of the lady in his crime contrasts with the lack of attention he accorded her elsewhere. Viaud told nothing of her background, not even how she looked. Implicating her does not, of course, excuse him. Had Viaud been capable of the chivalric conduct of the "gentleman" Swettenham took him for, he would have assumed the sole guilt for murder and cannibalism.

Civilized, restrained, reasonable, orderly, artificial, elegant, tasteful, enlightened: these are the adjectives that historians like to apply to the eighteenth century. Even the savage business of war was allegedly tamed, made subject to rules specified by Grotius and Vattel. A favorite anecdote illustrating the eighteenth-century concern for form over emotion is that of the British officer at the Battle of Fontenoy, who invited his French counterpart to have his men fire first.[50] The rational, restrictive society thus depicted was always more of an ideal than a reality. At best, it applied to a minor segment of the people of western Europe

---

50. In fact it was less an instance of politeness than application of a standard tactic for military advantage (Christopher Duffy, *The Military Experience in the Age of Reason* [New York: Atheneum, 1988], p. 212).

and of some transplanted centers of European culture overseas. Of these, North America was most notable. Bernard Bailyn sees it, at this period before the American Revolution, as "the exotic far western periphery, a marchland of the metropolitan European culture system."[51]

Viaud and his companions were blown beyond this marchland, farther than the remotest outposts of French and British civilization. There was nothing artificial about the environment in which they found themselves, and the lack of artifacts killed most of them. They were face to face with Nature at its most niggardly and least benign. Nothing could have been more unnatural than the contemporary cult of the so-called "natural" practiced by Versailles courtiers fired up by Rousseau's operetta *Le Devin du Village*. It was not Rousseau's state of nature but that described in Hobbes's *Leviathan* with which Viaud and his companions had to grapple. It was nasty and brutish for all of them, and short for most of them, but initially it was not solitary.

At the time of the shipwreck, there was a great deal of unity among the band. They cooperated, apparently amicably, under some direction from Viaud, with the result that all got off the wreck of *Le Tigre* onto Dog Island. Thereafter both unity and discipline deteriorated. The Indian Antonio split up the party. Captain La Couture, the nominal leader, and Viaud, the apparent natural leader, should not have allowed themselves to be in the same segment, but even in their group, discipline was lost to the point where its members, while fearful of theft in the night, organized no system of sentinels. The groups became further fragmented and, as individuals, in pairs, or trios, more and more of them perished.

It is impossible to determine whether Antonio was the unmitigated villain that Viaud depicts. It is conceivable, even likely, that the castaways gave him cause for resent-

51. Bernard Bailyn, *The Peopling of British North America: An Introduction* (New York: Knopf, 1986), p. 112.

ment; that, for instance (and despite Viaud's assertion of his willingness), Antonio had no voice in the sailors' appropriation of his hut for their living quarters (p. 56). What is sure is that neither of two eighteenth-century stereotypes, those of the noble savage and the enlightened European, fit the behavior of Antonio and the castaways. If Antonio marooned the seafarers to steal their guns, the sailors showed even more brutality in killing Antonio's family to acquire its pirogue.

And yet, it is in this descent of Europeans into savagery that the justification for reproducing this old book may lie. It is true that it is one of the very few contemporary accounts of the Gulf Coast of Florida in the 1760s that exists, but in this respect, its value is largely vitiated by Viaud's vagueness. He was not a biologist, cartographer, or geographer, although he truly, if imprecisely, succeeds in conveying an impression of wild desolation: "Our gaze wandered all around us, even scanning the far distance, but discovered nothing promising. We stood on a ridge. On all sides we saw a boundless skyline. On our right was the sea and our left a forest stretching as far as the eye could see. In front of us, in the direction we had determined to go, was a dry empty plain on which could be seen only the traces of wild beasts" (p. 90).

Of more value is the way in which Viaud showed how the wilderness beyond the colonial periphery could cause Europeans to disintegrate in every respect.

To a large extent we derive our ideas of America before the Revolution from the writings of men in organizations — church, army, representative assembly, plantation, college, or business. Viaud and his companions faced the wilderness entirely dependent on their own resources. Materially, they were exiguous. Essentially, all they could rely on were character and intelligence, of which, despite his braggadocio, Viaud probably had the most.

Initially he saw himself as a man of reason. *"Ecoutez la*

raison!" he commands his fellow castaways, and they obey (p. 49), ceasing to crowd the frail craft which alone can take them from the wreck of *Le Tigre*. When he returns to the ship to salvage usable items, a task for which helpers would have seemed wise, he prefers to go alone (p. 51), because he was thinking clearly. He did not want the timidity of the sailors to affect his own resolution. In addition (although the point is not made in *Naufrage*), to demand that unwilling sailors accompany him would have been to put his assumed authority over them to a test that it might have failed. By going alone he enhanced his prestige and his power to command the sailors which endured, at least for a time. They allowed him, surely with some reluctance, to destroy their barrels of rum (p. 53), and he dissuaded them from their scheme of killing Indians. His arguments were purely pragmatic and rational, containing not a jot of moral persuasion (p. 56). Soon afterward, however, hardship had so rotted his rational faculty that he favored a murderous plot similar to the one he had denounced (p. 58). Desclau and La Couture made him desist, not because he accepted their reasoning, but because he had to have their help for his scheme to succeed. An accurately fulfilled premonition convinced Viaud that reason alone could not solve all problems. Subsequently he became convinced that belief in chimeras, however contrary to reason (p. 64), could have benefit—either in perpetuating hope, and hence the struggle to survive, or in producing swift death through supernatural intervention (pp. 45,86,108–9). Both alternatives were preferable to the despair and slow, painful death dictated by reason as the fate of the castaways.

One by one, the party to which Viaud belonged grew smaller. More and more, as physical deterioration continued, Viaud ceased to think. He acted on impulse, most egregiously in killing his slave. If tried in a modern court for the crime, he would certainly have pleaded "temporary insanity," since he admitted to regret when, having eaten, some of his reasoning powers returned (p. 96). A prosecuting attorney, however, could have used the evidence of *Naufrage* to show that he had seriously contemplated a murder when he was suffering from frustration and hunger, less extreme motivations than starvation (p. 58).

Other examples show the erosion of the power of Viaud's mind to control his actions. Viaud knew, for instance, that there was no sense in looking for his lost flint at night, but could not stop himself from doing so (p. 101). There is little evidence that Viaud took Madame La Couture's opinions into account. Despite his use of *nous,* it was probably Viaud himself who made the unfortunate decision (p. 90) to veer inland. His companion realized that the seashore offered the best prospect of finding food (p. 108). Eventually she was able to act on some of her opinions because he could no longer prevent her. Viaud had reached the limit of his moral, intellectual, and finally physical resources. His legs could no longer carry him and he could not speak. He lost even the impulse to survive, falling into that deep calm, comparable to the state between sleeping and waking (p. 108), which was the prelude to death. In that condition, when he heard the cries of (he thought) Indians, even he, like some of his shipmates previously, did not care whether they saved him or killed him. The realization that the strangers were not Indians reanimated him. He found just enough strength to make the effort that resulted in his rescue.

Viaud was no literary artist. But despite the flaws in the narrative, and in the man himself, his *Naufrage* is a unique and neglected contribution, not so much to the history of British East Florida, as to an understanding of the human experience beyond the farthest boundary of colonial civilization.

Robin F. A. Fabel
Auburn, Alabama

Naufrage et Aventures de M. Pierre Viaud

Natif de Bordeaux, Capitaine de Navire

Histoire véritable, vérifiée sur
l'Attestation de Mr. Sevettenham,
Commandant du Fort St. Marc des Appalaches

Bordeaux
1768

Editor's Note

We have published M. Viaud's adventures for the benefit of upright and sensitive readers who will be shocked by the dreadful misfortunes which he endured for eighty-one days, from 16 February to 8 May 1766. It is almost impossible to imagine how a man could have survived such a terrible ordeal.

Although its truth may be thought questionable, everything related in Viaud's narrative is supported by others. M. Viaud is currently very much alive and respected by those who know him. His reliability and competence in the maritime service have earned him the trust of several merchants. He dares to publish his adventures under his own name because he wrote them himself. Only a few words and some expressions have been changed out of deference to those sensitive readers who might be offended by his simple, sometimes crude, sailor's style. But we have meticulously kept his ideas and afterthoughts and his way of expressing them. To drastic rewriting we have preferred his nautical roughness, if we may put it that way, which is not, perhaps, without virtue and which possesses, above all, an open and sincere tone which will surely be read with pleasure. We are leaving elegance and genteelness to novelists who need them to compensate readers for the vapidity of their offerings. Without these affectations what impact could the poorly-imagined actions of their fictional heroes achieve? They may interest young people of undemanding taste who devour that kind of literature, but mature readers scorn and ignore it. The misfortunes of M. Viaud do not need these odd embellishments. You will not find here the story of his life, but only the tale of his shipwreck and the horrors which followed. M. Pierre Viaud is a ship's captain and was recognized as such by the admiralty at Marennes in October 1761.

FOR A LONG TIME, MY FRIEND, you worried about my fate. Together with my family you thought that I had probably died on my last voyage. The time which passed without my writing confirmed you in that belief. But my letter, you say, ended the anguish caused by the thought of my death. The grief of my friends flatters and moves me. It consoles me for my past ordeal and I rejoice that I am still alive to taste once more the pleasure of being loved.

You complain that I was satisfied to state that I had been shipwrecked without giving any details. Now that you have been reassured about my life and health, you want a fuller account of my adventures. I do not want to refuse you anything, but it is a painful undertaking which I shall not complete except with difficulty. I cannot recall without shuddering the misfortunes I have endured. I am amazed that I survived them. Not many men have experienced similar blows. Some of them will arouse pity in a soul as sensitive as yours, but others will inspire horror. You will see how deep was the despair into which my sufferings plunged me and it will not surprise you at all that they exhausted my physical strength, weakened my mental balance, and that my terrible situation often prevented me from being reasonable. Above all do not expect me to order this tale meticulously. I have no exact recollection of most of the dates. How could they impress themselves on my mind when I was overwhelmed by the severest suffering? My torments grew worse on succeeding days: on each of them my misery affected me too sharply to allow me to brood on the trials of the previous day. For almost two months my soul knew no feeling but pain. The frenzy and rage of despair seemed to deprive it of all other feeling. Decades were almost completely wiped from my memory and I was aware only of my suffering. I shall narrate the actual facts, without adornment and without artifice: to keep a friend's interest they are unnecessary. I am unused to writing, so do not look for stylistic elegance. You will find only a sailor's work, very frank but full of faults.

When I left Bordeaux in February 1765, on the ship *Aimable Suzette,* commanded by M. Saint Cric, for whom I served as mate, I was not expecting the misfortunes which fate was preparing for me in the New World. The voyage was successful and I arrived at St. Domingue without experiencing any kind of accident. I shall not discuss my stay on the island; business affairs filled every moment. Finally I was able to concern myself with my return to France. The time for it drew near, and its date was already decided, when I fell ill a few days before I was due to embark. I was annoyed by this development but, in the belief that the climate of St. Domingue was responsible for my sickness, I persuaded myself that I would recover as soon as I left the island. This consoling idea made me long for the day of departure. It finally came, but did not provide the hoped-for improvement. In fact the sea and ship's lurching made me worse. I was told that to continue my voyage would be dangerous, an opinion confirmed by my persistent weakness. I was compelled to agree to return to dry land and disembarked in November on the Caye de St. Louis. This necessity was the source of my misfortunes.

Several days of rest on St. Louis and the generous care of M. Desclau, a resident of the islet who gave me lodging in his house, soon restored my health. With keen impatience I waited for a chance to return to Europe, for I knew that a long stay on St. Louis would exhaust my stock of money. My host, M. Desclau, was aware of this concern and that I was devoured by boredom. I fully recognized the generosity with which he had helped me during my illness and we became the firmest of friends. I could not hide from him the cause of my discontent. He understood completely, and did everything he could to make me feel better.

One day he approached me with the following proposal: "I have been thinking about your situation. The only thing the matter with you is the fear of remaining here a long time with nothing to do. The reason you want to go back to France without delay is the prospect of a job. You still have some funds. Try your luck. You could triple them. I regularly sail to Louisiana with merchandise I am certain to sell. The product that I get there for the return trip also brings me a decent profit.[1] I know this trade. I've done this kind of thing many times. Come with me. One day you will thank me for the advice I am giving you."

In the situation I was in, I had nothing better to do. Friendship prompted M. Desclau's offer and I did not hesitate to accept it. I became his partner and invested in his venture. We made the necessary purchases, concerning which he helped me with impressive zeal and the strictest honesty. We chartered a brigantine, *Le Tigre,* commanded by M. La Couture. Loading the cargo was completed with all possible speed and on embarkation we numbered sixteen: the captain, his wife and son, the brigantine's mate, nine sailors, M. Desclau, a black slave I had bought to be my servant, and myself.

We set sail from the roadstead of St. Louis on 2 January 1766, making our way toward Jeremie Inlet, where was a little port to the north of Cape Dame Marie and where we stopped for twenty-four hours. We left it to make for Petit Goave,[A] but this second leg of the voyage turned out less happily than the first. For twelve hours we endured a violent squall which would certainly have driven us onto the

---

A. As distinct from Grand Goave, which is four leagues to windward of Leogane, while Petit Goave is one league away from Grand Goave. Nobody would cast anchor except from dire necessity. [Notes at bottom of pages are Viaud's. Translator's numbered notes may be found at the end of the narrative.]

Cayes-mittes,[B] had the wind not somewhat abated, allowing us to sail away from those shores. If our skipper had
been a little more knowledgeable and a bit less obstinate,
we could have avoided this danger. From that moment I
began to realize that he had more talk than skill and I foresaw that our voyage was bound to end with some accident.
I promised myself to keep an eye on his actions to thwart,
if possible, the hazards to which his ignorance might expose
us.

Business affairs compelled us to spend three days at Petit
Goave. On leaving, we set course for Louisiana but almost
always the wind was adverse. On 26 January we sighted
Isla de Pinos,[C] which our captain insisted was Cape San Antonio.[2] I took a bearing and easily discovered he was mistaken, but tried in vain to show him that he was wrong.
His obstinacy prevented him from admitting it. He heed-
lessly continued on his course and steered us toward some
breakers. We were already among them when I noticed
them at night by the light of the moon. I wasted no time
in reproaches, but at last the captain began to feel that
he had been wrong not to trust me, and his fear, silencing
his pride, made him confess it. The danger was pressing.
I took the job of the mate who was very ill and in no condition to help. Controlling the maneuver myself, I put the
boat about as the only way to save our lives. We thus succeeded in evading one peril but found ourselves exposed
to a host of others.

Battered by the waves, our vessel was already taking
water in several places. Alarmed, the crew wanted me to
take charge of the navigation, but I had only a theoretical

B. Small islands in the vicinity of Hispaniola stretching from north to
south. They are part of the Antilles. [Viaud does not clarify effectively,
since all the westerly islands of the West Indies, including Cuba, Jamaica,
Puerto Rico, and Hispaniola itself are part of the Greater Antilles.]

C. This island is opposite the central part of western Cuba and is separated from it by a channel about four leagues wide.

knowledge of the coasts thereabout. I had never sailed them and I knew that my knowledge could never take the place of experience. What is more, I knew that the captain would be outraged; he could scarcely be denied the right to command his own vessel. To avoid giving him the right to make this complaint, I contented myself with closely watching his conduct, as much for my own peace of mind as for that of all the others, who now trusted nobody but me.

At last we rounded Cape San Antonio. Fresh gales struck us and opened the leaks again. Although they were in constant use, the two pumps contained them with difficulty. The wind was unrelentingly adverse and the weather worsened. The sea was rough and a violent storm threatened. We could not have survived it. Everyone on the ship was afraid. Any improvement in our sad and terrifying situation seemed unlikely, but in these dire circumstances, on 10 February, at seven in the evening, we met a Spanish frigate coming from Havana. She was carrying a governor and a senior military officer who were going to take possession of Louisiana for Spain and asked us to keep company with her.[3] We agreed with pleasure. Had we not been forestalled, we would have asked permission to follow her. During a tiring and troublesome voyage, nothing is more comforting to sailors than to meet a vessel sailing the same course. It is not that they can count on receiving much help in the middle of a storm, when everyone is too concerned with his own preservation to worry about others', but that an expected danger seems less menacing when one knows that it will be shared.

We did not manage to keep company with the frigate for very long. We lost her at night when she was making way under reduced sail, while we set no sails at all and were compelled to lie to. The following day we found ourselves alone, and, to increase our alarm, discovered a new leak. I was consulted about what we should do. I thought it vital to lighten the vessel at once. It is a harsh necessity for merchants to have to throw away part of the goods they have acquired with so much labor and in which they have invested money in the hope of making more. In circumstances like ours, however, preserving life is the first priority. It becomes the only concern, and all others are forgotten. I had all the heavy cargo thrown overboard. Since the two pumps were not coping, at the main hatch I set up a makeshift pump-well with barrels from our cargo, so that we could bail out the water with buckets. These measures proved useless. The water continued to gain on us. Their work exhausted the sailors without achieving its goal. It was impossible to hold back the sea much longer. We decided to put into Mobile. It was the nearest port but the wind's direction in fact gave us no other choice. At the time we were twelve or fifteen miles from the Chandeleur Islands.[4]

We therefore made course for Mobile, but Providence prevented our making landfall there because the wind changed direction after two hours, and we had to give up the attempt. Instead we made every effort to reach Pensacola, which was some distance from Mobile. This plan failed too. The winds continued to thwart us, deflected us again, and kept us in rough seas against which we still strove, lacking any hope of making any port whatsoever, just waiting for the moment when the ocean depths would open and swallow us up.

I have made many voyages in my life. I can remember none in which I suffered so much or had a worse run of luck. Never were Providence and the sea joined with more consistent violence to torment unhappy travelers. In the end we felt that saving our vessel and belongings was out of the question, and even saving our lives was moot. We concerned ourselves solely with preserving life and tried to strike the coast at Apalache,[5] but we could not make it. We stayed at the mercy of the waves, suspended between life and death, lamenting our bad luck, sure now that we would die, but never slackening our efforts to escape danger. Such was our condition from 12 February up to the 16th, when at seven in the evening we found ourselves grounded on a reef six miles from the mainland. The pounding of the breakers was so violent as to smash open the stern of our vessel. We remained for thirty minutes in this situation, experiencing inexpressible fear. After half an hour the shocking force of the waves threw us beyond the reef. We found ourselves afloat again with no rudder and at the mercy of both the sea which surrounded us and of the constantly rising water entering our vessel.

Until then we had managed to hold onto a scrap of hope. Now it vanished completely. Our vessel resounded to the pathetic cries of sailors making their farewells, preparing for death with prayers for God's pardon, interrupting them to make vows, in spite of the dreadful certainty that they would never live to fulfill them. What a scene, my friend! Only a witness could have any idea of it. What I have outlined is very imperfect, and much less poignant than its reality.

I shared the crew's terror. My despair showed less, but I was every whit as frightened. The excess of bad luck, and the feeling that it was unavoidable, gave me a kind of stability. I accepted the fate awaiting me as unalterable. I abandoned my life to the being who gave it me, but retained enough courage to anticipate the fatal moment coolly, and to concern myself with ways of delaying it.

My apparent calm communicated itself to the crew. At that terrifying time I inspired them with a kind of trust which made them ready to obey my commands. The wind was pushing us toward the shore. I steered with the foresail braces and sheets, and by extraordinary luck, which we had no right to expect, we arrived at nine in the evening east of Dog Island and ran aground within musket shot of the land.[6] The sea's roughness did not allow us to reach it. We thought of chopping up our masts to make a raft which could carry us there. While we were engaged in this task, the violence of the wind and the force of the waves combined to hurl our brigantine onto its port side. This unforeseen jolt all but killed us. We should all have fallen into the sea and perished but narrowly avoided this fate. Some of our sailors, who were jerked into the water by the shock, had the good fortune to get back to the vessel and, thanks to the helping hands we extended, to climb on board again.

Suddenly the moon which, until that moment, had provided us with a feeble light often interrupted by clouds, disappeared from sight altogether. Once deprived of the benefit of moonlight, it became impossible for us to think of crossing to dry land. We had to steel ourselves to wait for day on the side of our vessel. The night seemed endless. We were exposed to heavy rain: the sky appeared to turn to water. The waves rose higher by the minute, swamping our boat and bursting over us. Thunder rolled from every point of the compass. From time to time, lightning flashes showed us an endless horizon and a raging sea ready to engulf us. The ensuing darkness became even more terrifying.

Clinging to the side of our vessel, nailed, as it were, to anything we had been able to lay hands on, rain-soaked, numb with cold, worn out by our efforts to resist the impetuous waves, which would have dragged us away, at last we saw dawn break. It clarified the dangers we had endured and which still beset us. The sight we beheld seemed even more frightening. We saw dry land a short distance away, but could not get there. The wildness of the sea, whose waves crashed with a fury I have seldom seen, deterred even the bravest of swimmers. Any unfortunate wretch who exposed himself to such waves would have risked either being carried out to the open sea or being smashed against the boat or the rocky shore. On seeing them, despair seized our sailors. Their plaintive and doleful cries increased. Thunder claps and the howling of the wind agitating the ocean could not stifle their wails and, combining with them, added to the horror of the situation.

Several hours passed without bringing any change in our

lot. A sailor[D] who from daybreak had wept incessantly and who had shown himself weaker than his comrades, suddenly stopped crying and, after a deep silence of several minutes, got up at last with unusual vivacity.

"What are waiting for?" he shouted with desperate determination. "Death surrounds us on all sides. It will soon come for us all. Let's fly to meet it. Let us speed its leisurely blows. We must find death in the waves. Perhaps if we go to meet it, death will retreat. Land lies in front of us. It's reachable. I am going to try. If I fail, all I'm doing is to hasten my end by a few hours and to shorten the length of my misery."

With these words he dove into the sea. Fired by his example, several sailors wanted to follow him. I only just managed to hold them back by pointing to their shipmate, tossed by the waves, uselessly fighting them. First he was swept to the beach and actually touched it, but was then dragged back by the sea, in which he vanished for several minutes. When he came up again, we saw him crushed against a rock. This cruel sight made the sailors shudder and rid them of all impulse to copy his action.

Most of the day had passed. It was five in the evening. We thought with terror of the night that we had already spent, and we trembled in anticipation of the one to follow. The waves had carried off the masts and shrouds we had cut down the previous evening. The hope of using a raft to save ourselves had vanished. We had a rowboat in bad repair, but it was too dilapidated to make the short crossing from the brigantine to the shore. We had examined it on several occasions, but each time we had given up the idea of using it. Three sailors, braver or more desperate than the rest, dared to set out in this frail craft. They got into it without telling anyone what they were about. We did not realize their intention until after they had pushed off, but believed them as good as dead.

D. This sailor was Dutch.

We watched their struggles and the difficulties they overcame, while constantly risking being swamped. In spite of our expectations, they reached the shore. We envied their success and all regretted that we had lacked their boldness. Everyone complained because they had given no warning of their plan. If ever the sight of happiness was mortifying to the miserable it was then. Their gestures to us and their demonstrations of glee stabbed us. Their good luck made us feel our bad luck more keenly. No doubt what I am telling you is horrible and inhuman. Nevertheless this despicable feeling is natural. I admit that it is discreditable. All the same, I say to those who condemn it and consider us as monsters for harboring it, "Let them first put themselves in our position, and then let them judge us."

Soon darkness hid our more fortunate companions from sight. With no choice but to remain with our vessel, we compared our predicament unfavorably with theirs. Our sufferings seemed worse, because they were not sharing them. This second night proved as testing as the one before. The strain was the same, but the exhaustion we felt from lack of sleep scarcely left us the strength to cope with it.

Ever since our vessel had been blown on its side, we had been unable to get inside her. We had not dared to make holes in her for fear of creating gaps for water to enter which, filling up the vessel, would soon have broken her apart. Thus would we have been deprived of our only refuge. Consequently we had no provisions and no way of getting them. We had survived all this time without eating or drinking.

It seemed that God had taken pleasure in heaping on us every kind of misfortune. Our weary bodies vainly craved rest and food to restore their strength. Both were denied. Never had we anticipated death in such a hideous way. Our wrecked brigantine was held in place by huge rocks. The waves dashed against her with appalling force which shook and constantly threatened to shatter her and submerge us. Luckily for us she remained intact.

The following day, 18 February, we witnessed the break of a day we had despaired of ever living to see. Death would have relieved us of our suffering and would no doubt have been a blessing, but the strongest sentiment in the human heart is love of life. Mankind clings to it to the very end. The torments people endure can weaken but rarely quite extinguish it. On seeing that we were still on the side of the brigantine, our first action was to thank God for having allowed us to live and to pray that He would complete His work and crown His mercy by providing a means of reaching dry land.

Never was a prayer more heartfelt, and God seemed to grant it. The wind abated, the raging sea calmed, and we were presented with a sight which, though terrible enough, was much less so than on preceding days. One of our sailors, an excellent swimmer, after gazing for some time at the route he would have to take to reach the beach, decided to make the attempt. "I am going to rejoin my shipmates," he told us. "We'll try to caulk and frap[7] the rowboat. Maybe we'll make her stout enough to make several trips back and save all your lives. It's our only chance. Let's not argue about it. We are getting weaker all the time. Let's not wait until we are totally worn out. Let's use our small remaining strength to get ourselves out of this horrible mess."

We backed his suggestion and, as best we could, helped him to carry out his scheme. It was the only one which could be of any use to us. We gave him handkerchiefs and ten fathoms[8] of rope which might be used to caulk the rowboat. Loading himself with them, he jumped into the sea. Several times we saw him on the point of sinking. Our anxious eyes followed his every move. We saw in him our only resource, our only possible savior. We shared his risks; our fate depended on him. We urged him on with shouts and gestures, mentally struggling alongside him. We suffered when he had to make an extra effort to overcome the resistance of waves. Our imagination and urgent wishes put us in his place. We experienced what he experienced. We over-

came the breakers or were beaten by their fury, and grew
weary as much as he. We begged God to help him; his
safety became ours. At last, after a hundred alternating
bouts of fear and hope, we saw him, after unspeakable
effort, reach the shore. At once we fell to our knees to
thank God. A spark of joy flamed in our souls and warmed
them.

It was then seven in the morning. We waited impatiently
for the moment when someone would come to fetch us.
We stayed constantly facing the beach. Our eager eyes were
always darting there, looking at our four sailors busy
around the rowboat, missing not one of their actions insofar
as distance allowed it. Such lively and sustained observation seemed to soothe our impatience and to shorten our
time of waiting. Although we urged on their work with our
longing, it still progressed slowly, and we quaked inwardly
at the thought that it might all be futile. The work was
done at three o'clock in the afternoon. We saw the rowboat
launched into the water and it came toward our vessel.
How can I depict the joy of the crew at this sight? It burst
forth in the form of shouts and tears of happiness. Everyone
hugged whoever was next to him, congratulating him on
this sign of divine favor.

These feelings of tenderness and compassion for each
other did not last. Everything changed when it became a
question of who should go first. The small rowboat could
hold only part of our group. It would sink if everybody
climbed aboard. We all knew it, but no one wanted to risk
waiting for a second trip. The fear that some accident would
make a second trip for the rowboat impossible, stranding
those left on the brigantine, caused all the sailors to clamor
to be among the first passengers. The sailors rowing the
little boat urged me to take my chance in it at once, because
they feared it was not sturdy enough to make two ferrying
excursions. These words, which everyone heard, evoked yet
more groans and pleas of increased anguish for priority.

I swiftly asserted myself. Raising my voice, I commanded

silence. "Your shouting and fretting are pointless," I told everybody. "They do nothing but delay our rescue. Every one of you will die, if you insist on being ferried all at the same time. Listen to reason. Obey what reason commands, and then hope. We all run the same risks. In the situation we are in, giving preference to anyone is unacceptable. Misfortune makes us all equal. Let us choose by lot those who are to leave first. Accept what chance decides. To show the losers in the lottery that they have no reason to despair, I shall stay with them and be the last to leave the brigantine."

This suggestion amazed them, but they all agreed to it. By chance, a sailor had some playing cards in his pocket, and with this deck lots were cast. From the eleven we now numbered, four set off with the four sailors who had brought the rowboat to us. They arrived on land without incident, and the little craft came back to pick up others. While this was happening, I noticed that the force of the waves had all but detached the counter[E] from our vessel. Helped by Desclau and my black, I succeeded in breaking it off completely.[9] This flotsam seemed suitable to replace the rowboat as a means of getting to shore. I discussed it with Desclau, who agreed. When all the others had left in the rowboat, Desclau, my slave, and I got onto the counter, followed the rowboat, and arrived at the beach almost simultaneously with it.

How happy we were to be on dry land! What thanks we then offered to God! How sweet it was to stretch out on *terra firma*, without worrying that it would give way under us! By luck we found oysters on the banks of a nearby river.[10] They made a tasty meal. The hunger we had endured since 16 February provided the best possible seasoning for them. We reveled in our new situation, passing a peaceful night in deep sleep, which restored our strength and was undisturbed by concern for the future. The following morn-

E. A nautical term meaning all the exterior part of a vessel's poop.

ing we awoke with the same satisfied feeling. It did not last long.

Our ship's mate had fallen ill some days after we left port. The strain of the voyage, the lurching of the vessel, and the constant alarms which befell us had worsened his condition. When we were first wrecked, he scarcely had the strength to rise from his bed, and I am still astounded that he was strong enough to clamber onto the side of the vessel when the waves overset her. The ordeal which we then endured almost completely exhausted him. When it was a question of going into the rowboat, he was the first chosen in the lottery and he got into it without assistance. He seemed reanimated, but it was a dangerous exertion motivated by fear which, while giving him vigor for the occasion, drained his final reserves. He was the only member of the crew to spend a troubled night on shore. He had the fortitude to suffer without complaint, because he did not want to wake us. When daylight dragged us from the grip of sleep, I went to him and found him extremely weak. I shouted for help, and everyone came, but what could we do? "My final hour has come," he told us. "I thank God for sparing me until I could see all of you safe. That worry, at least, will not accompany me to my grave. May you profit, friends, from the favors which God is granting you! You may not yet have seen the end of your woes, but I like to think that you have survived the worst of them. I won't be sharing them with you any more. Pray for me . . . I am dying."

With these words he lost consciousness and, a moment later, he breathed his last breath. His going brought tears to our eyes and put an end to our self-satisfaction. It made us consider our situation soberly. We were on an uninhabited island. The mainland was not far away, but was apparently inaccessible.

We were anxious to render the last rites to our mate.[F]

F. His name was Dutronche.

We buried him in his clothes and dug his grave in the sand. After completing this respectful, doleful ceremony, we walked along the seashore, where we found some of our trunks, several barrels of rum, and a number of bales of merchandise which the sea had cast up and which must have reached shore before us. Except for the rum, in our opinion this jetsam was worth very little. We would have preferred a little ship's biscuit,[11] firearms for defense and hunting, and, above all, fire. We sadly missed a means of making fire to dry our clothes and limbs numbed by cold air and seawater. Heat was our keenest need. Our imaginations concentrated totally on a means to satisfy it. We tried in vain the Indian method of rubbing two sticks together, but failed through lack of skill.

Just as, finally, we gave up all hope of starting a fire, I noticed that an almost perfect calm had descended on the sea. I decided to go back to the brigantine in the rowboat. Even if it chanced to sink, the crossing was short, I knew how to swim, and the now gentle waves posed no great danger. I tried to persuade one or two of the sailors, excellent swimmers, to come with me, but they recoiled from the mere suggestion. They remembered what they had suffered on the brigantine's side, and blenched at the prospect of going there without hope, should the sea turn rough, of returning to land. I did not think fit to insist. They might still have refused but, even if they did decide to come with me, gripped the whole time by fear, trembling at the swelling of the smallest wave, they would have been of no help, and would have done nothing but get in my way and hamper my undertaking. The very thought of our vessel frightened everybody. Some of them tried to dissuade me from continuing with my project. I had no time for this panicky terror. Suddenly I ran to get into the rowboat, wanting to hear nothing lest the chorus of warnings sap my will. In a number of situations in which I have found myself, I have seen how the example of the majority can dominate the individual. Among cowards a brave soldier loses his nerve, just as a coward absorbs courage from his comrades. I arrived safely at the brigantine. In subsiding, the sea had partially cleared a hatchway. I moored the rowboat there and, with some difficulty, forced an entry. Inside was a great deal of water, in some places chest-high. It was not easy to find what I was looking for; everything was topsy-turvy. By a lucky chance, under my hand I found a small cask containing about twenty-five pounds of gunpowder. It was in a spot above the level of the water. It would have been difficult anyhow for water to penetrate that particular barrel. It was well seasoned and of a kind normally used to hold brandy but where our captain had kept his gunpowder. I seized it along with six muskets, a number of silk handkerchiefs,[12] some wool blankets and a bag holding thirty-five to forty pounds of ship's biscuit.[13] I also found two axes. In all, it was as much as I could take back.

I returned to the island with my small cargo. It was received with general joy. I had the others collect a great pile of dry wood, of which there was an abundance on the beach, and lit a large fire.[14] It was an unbelievable blessing for our little group. We busied ourselves with drying the clothes we wore, the blankets I had found, and some of the garments from our trunks. I immediately told some sailors to get water from the river to soak our biscuit, which the sea had almost completely ruined. The river water was a little salty, but drinkable. We improved it with rum, but we made do with it, because we did not think that the island could provide us with better water.[G]

While some men occupied themselves with soaking our biscuit and then laying it out to dry, others cleaned the six muskets, and soon made them serviceable. In my trunk I had a few pounds of lead shot. Together with some powder, I gave it to our two best shots. They went hunting and, at the end of an hour, brought back five or six head of

---

G. We were mistaken. Dog island is watered by a great many rivers, but we did not know it and we stayed close to the beach were we first landed.

the kind of game which abounds on this coast. We cooked them and that evening had excellent game-soup. We then turned in, sleeping the night away near our fire, wrapped in dry blankets. Compared to sleeping warm, the other comforts we enjoyed seemed minor.

The following day, 20 February, we thought about what we had to do. The change from a desperate to a somewhat improved condition and the occupations of the previous day had given us no time to look ahead. We had thought ourselves lucky to escape the shipwreck, but reflecting on what lay ahead ended our complacency. We were on an unpeopled island. There was no beaten path to lead us to a settlement. We would have to cross extremely wide rivers and go through thick, inaccessible forests, in which it would be easy to get lost. There were encounters with wild beasts to fear and, certainly as perilous, meetings with Indians. We did not know if there were any of them on Dog Island at the time. We knew that the Indians living on the Apalache coast left their villages in winter, in order to live on the neighboring islands, where they hunted until April, before going home to the mainland. They would take with them the hides of the animals they had killed and would then trade them with Europeans for the guns, powder, and brandy[15] which they needed. It could happen that we would be surprised by a sizable party of Indians at a time when we were not at all expecting them. They might take our lives to get hold of our pathetic remaining belongings. We were also afraid that the casks of taffia,[16] which were on the beach, might fall into their hands. These primitive people who love rum would probably get drunk. Then, meeting us in that condition, when making them listen to reason would be impossible, they might massacre us all without mercy. We did not hesitate to eliminate this dangerous eventuality by staving in the barrels. We saved only three, hiding them in a wood and, for greater security, burying them in sand.[17]

We spent the whole of that day and the one following

with the foreboding which imagining these possibilities was bound to inspire. We were constantly nervous. From fear of Indian attack we did not dare split up. We were on guard day and night against a surprise assault, keeping watch in all directions. Some, doubting the competence of whoever was assigned as sentry, interrupted their own sleep to be awake at the same time. Among such a small number of people, I have never seen so much misery and timidity.

On the morning of 22 February, worn out by the strain of the night, almost all of our group had finally given in to sleep. Two fearful sailors, whose eyes were still open, suddenly shouted, "Wake up! Here come the Indians! We are all dead men!"

Everybody jumped up at these words and, without further inquiry, prepared to run away. Eventually I managed to stop them and made them actually look at the Indians. They numbered five: two men and three women, each armed with a musket and a club.

"What have you got to worry about?" I asked. "Is this an unbeatable force? We're stronger, aren't we? We're in a position to dictate to them if they are unfriendly. Let's wait for them. Maybe they'll be useful and help us to leave this place."

My companions were ashamed of their panic and without fuss seated themselves near the fire. The Indians drew near. We received them with a great show of friendship. They responded in similar fashion. We gave them some of our belongings and cups of taffia, which they drank with gusto. Their leader spoke a little Spanish. One of our sailors, who understood the language, entered into conversation with him and acted as our interpreter.

We learned that the Indian was called Antonio, and that he came from St. Mark's, Apalache.[18] He had been wintering on an island about nine miles from the one we were on.[19] Wreckage from our ship, which the sea had cast on its beaches, had caused him to visit Dog Island. Those with him were his family: his mother, wife, sister, and nephew.

We asked him if he would take us to St. Mark's, telling him that we would make sure he would be rewarded. He withdrew to consider this proposal and discussed it for almost an hour with his family. It was then that we noticed that he repeatedly looked at our weapons, trunks, blankets, and other belongings. We did not know what to make of his long conference. We became a little suspicious of him, but his open manner, when he returned and offered to take us immediately, removed our doubts. Antonio said that we were only thirty miles from St. Mark's and he deceived us, because the true figure is seventy-eight,[20] but we did not know it. Perhaps if we had been better informed, this small breach of good faith would have put us on our guard.

Antonio left with our gifts. Three sailors had no hesitation in accompanying him. He promised to come back on the following day with his pirogue.[21] After a fashion he kept his word.[22] We saw him again on 24 February. He brought us a field duck and a roe. Because he arrived late in the day, we did not leave the island until the 25th. Having loaded the pirogue with some of our belongings, six of us climbed aboard: the small craft could take no more. Those left behind had insisted that I should be among the first to go, because they were confident that I would not forget them and that, if Antonio refused to go back for them, I would know how to make him do so.

The Indian put us ashore on the other island, where we found our three companions who had been Antonio's passengers on the previous day. After arrival, nothing seemed more urgent to me than to justify the confidence placed in me by the five sailors left on Dog Island. I implored our guide to fetch them with the remainder of our belongings, but could not persuade him to make the trip immediately. First of all he wanted to take us over to the mainland, he said. I absolutely refused. This obstinacy made me suspicious and I eventually forced him to yield. After two whole days of nagging, I talked him into setting off. On 28 February we were all together again, a source of great satisfaction. As long as we were separated we felt a sense of loss, for we had become like brothers. By common accord we helped and supported each other. Class distinctions had vanished. The captain and the common sailor were friends and equals. Nothing is firmer than the bonds forged by misfortune. Fourteen individuals became members of one family.[23]

As soon as we were reunited, I called on Antonio to keep his promise to carry us over to the mainland, but his initial enthusiasm had cooled a great deal. To avoid being pestered, he kept away from us. He would go hunting with his family all day, and, in the evening, he would not visit his cabin, which he had given up to us and where we lived. We were perplexed by his behavior. What did he want from us? Was he waiting for a chance to seize our belongings and then abandon us? This suspicion made us wary, and we kept such a close watch that robbing us was made impossible. Some of my companions, tired of delay, proposed a solution which was extremely violent but which, in fact, might have saved us from a great many calamities. Their suggestion was to kill the five Indians, take their canoe, and attempt to row it to Apalache. I argued them out of this dire plan, which was fraught with danger. Once the Indians of Antonio's tribe learned of their deaths, they would want to avenge them. None of us knew the islands and waters of the region, so how would we find the mainland?[24] Chance might have taken us there, but how provident was it to embark with no hope except one based on chance?[25] We stayed on this island for five days, fishing and hunting and, for fear of exhausting our supply, rationing ourselves to a daily ounce of biscuit. Finally we went looking for Antonio, found him, and, thanks to much begging and some presents, persuaded him to do what we wanted. He agreed to guide us. Once more our group had to split up, and on 5 March we loaded the pirogue with the bulk of our belongings. Six of us got on board: Desclau, myself and my black, La Couture, his wife, and her fifteen-year-old son.

That both these last had survived all the hardships of our ordeal was a marvel. Antonio and his wife came with us. The other three Indians stayed with our eight sailors, from whom we parted with great sorrow. We all experienced the same thought. Our hearts contracted, a tremor which seemed to tell us that we were taking our last farewells and that we would never see each other again.

This eagerly sought voyage, arranged in spite of so many obstacles, was to prove more deadly for us than the voyage resulting in our shipwreck. We had already endured many misfortunes, but fresh ones awaited us. It was then, my friend, that I had most need of my resolution and that it often failed me. You will find in what I am going to tell you unbelievable hardships and horrible occurrences, of which even the memory still makes me sweat.

Antonio had promised us that our voyage would last no longer than two days and we had made our preparations accordingly. Fear of accidents, however, had caused us to take food for four days. It comprised six or seven pounds of biscuit, and several pieces of bear meat and smoked venison. This reasonable prudence proved inadequate. Our journey was going to be longer than four days, as we realized on the very first of them. After traveling nine miles, Antonio stopped and made us disembark on another island, where he compelled us to remain until the following day, on which we made no better progress. I noticed that instead of transporting us toward the mainland, he was amusing himself by taking us from one island to another.[H] This meandering disturbed me and increased my mistrust of Antonio's behavior. These small island-to-island trips used up six days. Our food was exhausted. We lacked all nourishment except the oysters we came across, and scraps

H. These islands are little known. When seen from the open sea, they seem to from part of the mainland but actually they are separated from it by a channel about six miles wide. I was set down on four of these islands, all of which are very flat and sandy.

of game which the Indian occasionally doled out to us.

In the days that followed, the way that Antonio organized our travel formed an unvarying pattern. We would
leave between eight and ten in the morning. At noon he
would make us halt until the following day. We often made
these stops in wretched places, where there was nothing
to eat, and at times nothing to drink either.

Thus we journeyed for seven days. We never reached the
object of our desires, the mainland, which was supposed
to be the whole purpose of our voyage. We were overcome
with weariness, worn down with malnutrition. We became
so weak that we were almost incapable of rowing. Our cruel
predicament affected me in a fashion I had never experienced. Our prolonged misfortunes made me furious and
soured my personality. I could see Antonio as nothing but
a wily rogue who wanted to turn our plight to his own advantage and who would callously let us die. This conviction
interfered with my rest and kept me awake one night, as
I lay near a huge fire we had lit, around which my companions lay sleeping. I called out for Desclau and La Couture,
with whom I had shared the sinister obsessions which
gripped me. I tried to persuade them to accept my conviction of what we might expect from the treacherous Indian.
I said that what he had already done justified my distrust.
I told them plainly what he wanted from us, and that he
would get it, if we did not strike first. I cannot now imagine
how I was able to insist with so much certainty on the need
to kill Antonio: after all, on the second island which we
visited, I was the one who stopped the sailors from murder-
ing him. I was not born a barbarian, but now distress had
made me ferocious, quite capable of meditating and committing murder. Our dilemma gave me an excuse and, in
my eyes, what immediately followed completely justified
my determination.

Desclau and La Couture would not agree to my plan.
They repeated the same arguments I had used to dissuade

the sailors. They did not convince me, but I yielded to their protests, and passed the rest of the night with them, without deciding on action.

The following day, 12 March, we went another six miles and, as usual, disembarked on an island. Sunk in misery and desperate for sleep, we each took a blanket in which, according to our custom, we wrapped ourselves and lay around a large fire. Sleep summoned us and we readily obeyed, for the more we slept, the less time we had to dwell on our misery. My sleep was short, however. My former disquiet returned more strongly than ever. The quickening of my blood gave me no rest. Morbid ideas flooded my imagination. I do not know if one should believe in presentiments. Perhaps they are a mere fancy that philosophy has destroyed, along with many other superstitions. It is a subject on which I shall not digress. I shall simply state what I experienced. I thought I saw myself by the seashore, from where I watched Antonio and his wife heading out to sea in his pirogue. My imagination was so forcefully struck by this vivid image that I yelled aloud, waking my companions. They came to me and asked if I were having a fit. I told them of my vision. They scoffed at such fantasies. Their comments and jokes convinced me that I had merely been dreaming. I was too far from the beach to see clearly what I had imagined took place there. In the end, I was laughing with the others about what had just happened. They lost no time in going back to sleep. I too let myself fall into a deep slumber, but at midnight awoke with a start, plagued with the same notion which had evoked such mockery a few hours before.

My uneasiness was deeper than ever. I could not stop myself from going to see what was happening on the beach. I got up silently without waking anybody and staggered to the seashore. The sky was cloudless. The moon shone with a constant brilliance which helped me see clearly. I looked at the place where the pirogue should have been.

I could not see it. I looked wildly around in every direction: it had disappeared. I called out Antonio's name. There was no reply. Awakened by my shouts, my companions ran to the shore. I had no need to tell them what had happened. They complained bitterly, groaning with regret for having stayed my hand the night before, when I wanted to pre-empt the schemes of the shifty Indian, although regrets are useless when irreparable harm has already been done.

Thus, for a second time, we found ourselves alone on a desolate island, without help and lacking both food and the weapons needed to obtain it. We had only the clothes on our backs and our blankets. Our muskets and other be-longings were in the pirogue. On that particular day we had left in it even the swords which customarily we kept with us. Our entire stock of offensive and defensive weap-ons consisted of a blunt knife which happened to be in my pocket. No one else in our group had one. On the island grew no roots or fruit which we could eat and the sea pro-vided no shellfish there. A dreadful situation! What future was there for us? And how could we summon the courage to maintain hope when there was every reason to abandon it?

As soon as day broke we gathered up our blankets, which were all the possessions left to us. We went to the seashore in the dubious hope of finding some oysters to appease our hunger. Our search was futile. We walked for a couple of hours without spying anything edible, nor even a drop of drinkable water.

When at length we reached the end of this island, we sighted another which was separated from the one we were on by a strait less than seven hundred yards wide. We had spent a night and a day there with the Indian. I remem-bered that it had excellent shellfish and good water. How we regretted that we had not been sooner marooned on it! At least we might have survived. This realization added to our grief. We sat on the sand, our eyes fixed on this at-tractive island, and bemoaned the limitations of our own.

After we had rested for some time, hunger gnawed us, and we discussed the risks of crossing the arm of the sea separating the two islands. Since death awaited us if we did not chance it, nobody objected. As we were about to start, we were delayed by a consideration which we had previously ignored. How could Madame La Couture and her son follow us? The crossing did not daunt seafaring men but it was extraordinarily perilous for a woman and a youth. We had already noticed that Monsieur La Couture was worried as he visually measured the strait and puzzled over a way of safely leading his loved ones over it. Humanity forbade us to leave them behind. We offered to take turns in literally lending a hand to them both while my black, the shortest of our group, would walk ahead testing the footing and warning us of places where it was uneven.[26]

I held Madame La Couture's hand while Desclau took her son's. Captain La Couture made two bundles, one from our blankets and another from clothes which we chose not to wear. He loaded one on my black's head and kept the other himself. We set out and found the going underfoot sufficiently firm and even. At its greatest depth the water reached only to our midriffs: moving slowly through it, we reached the other side. During this painful crossing Madame La Couture showed surprising strength and courage. She would consistently demonstrate these qualities and no one can allege that her presence was ever a hindrance or an embarrassment.

Once arrived at this island, where we hoped to find food, we experienced another inconvenience which might have proved fatal. We had spent an hour and a half in the water and we were gripped by cold as soon as we left it. We could not make a fire to dry and warm ourselves because we lacked the means to start one. There was not a single stone either on this island nor on those where we had previously stopped.

We felt the cold keenly. Only if we jumped up and down and kept constantly on the move could we manage to be warm. With the same motive we walked for hours looking for oysters, which were gulped down as soon as we found them. Once they had appeased our hunger, we made a small stock of them at a freshwater spring where we made camp. There we rested when the sun's warmth made it possible for us to stay still for a time without suffering from the dreaded cold. It also dried our damp clothes, sparing us enormous discomfort after dusk, but dry clothes alone could not ensure a restful night. The cold awoke us several times. We had no way of keeping it at bay except by getting up and walking about.

The following day the wind blew from the south and southeast, which helped to warm us. We went looking for shellfish by the shore. The sea was high, we found nothing and were compelled to feed on those collected the previous day. We would notice that, when the wind blew from that quarter, the sea never ebbed and that it was always necessary to build up a stock of shellfish before the tide turned. We acquired this lore painfully, after experiencing several days with nothing to eat. We had to forage among herbs and roots for anything which might conceivably replace shellfish. We could use only one plant, the small barberry,[27] a type of wood sorrel.

I shall not linger on what we did for the first ten days after Antonio marooned us. We had much to endure: cold March nights and sometimes hunger. We spent entire days looking for anything that could be eaten, cursing our luck and asking God to end our torment. Our condition remained unchanged, and details of our afflictions, complaints, and worries would make monotonous reading for you. It would be pointless for me to dwell on them.

On 22 March or thereabouts, for I cannot be certain about the dates which now follow, while complaining as usual and dreaming of ways of escaping our dismal refuge, someone recalled that on the beach of a neighboring island where our Indian had taken us was a derelict pirogue. We speculated that perhaps it would be possible to refit it and use it to cross the strait separating us from the mainland. This plan captivated us. The hope which it inspired might prove fanciful but we embraced it with as much zeal as if its realization was certain. The desperate are blind to difficulties. In the schemes they devise they see only the end of their woes. It is this goal which dominates their calculations. The circumstances which can prevent them getting there, and the inevitable obstacles which they will find confronting them, make little impression. They hotly reject them with contempt, refusing to examine them from fear that they might result in the abandonment of the pleasing idea consoling them.

So it was that Desclau, La Couture, and I concentrated on ways of getting near the old pirogue. We oriented ourselves as best we could. We mentally mapped the route we would have to take to reach the island. We guessed, in fact correctly, that we were no more than twelve or fifteen miles from it. We were not totally blind to the difficulties which would attend this journey. We expected to have to cross rivers and a saltwater strait but were undeterred and decided to attempt the undertaking, certain that, if it were at all possible, we could carry it out. We got under way on the very day that we made our decision. We did not want to take Madame La Couture and her son with us. They would only slow us down since they could not stand hardships and exhaustion as we could.[28] We might have been forced to leave them behind us on the banks of some unfordable river which could only be crossed by swimmers. Madame La Couture understood our reasons and agreed to stay behind with her lad. I left them my black as servant. On parting, we promised to return to them immediately, either with the pirogue, if we could refit it, or without it, if it could not be made serviceable or if we could not find it.

Our plan was our only hope, our last resort. We discussed

it as we traveled, talking of it as though its success were sure. This confidence revived our spirits, giving us fresh vigor and making our trek seem shorter. In all stages of life and in all circumstances men lull themselves with fantasies. They cease to content themselves with the enjoyment of real pleasures and conjure up imaginary ones. They become absorbed in illusion, a true blessing for those down on their luck, for they become so preoccupied that they feel their tribulations less keenly. They almost forget them.

After walking for three and a half hours we came to the tip of our island, having met with no river broad enough to delay us for any length of time. Those we saw would have been called small streams in Europe: we crossed them with ease. At the end of the island we found a kind of channel nearly a mile wide separating us from the island we were aiming at. The thought of crossing this stretch of water dismayed us as we assessed it with anxious eyes. The longing to get hold of a craft and the eagerness with which we strove to extricate ourselves from our plight kept us resolute. We sat down to rest for an hour, knowing we would need every ounce of our strength to succeed in the crossing we were about to undertake. We did not know if the channel would be totally fordable. We were concerned that, if it were not, the gaps which we would have to swim across might be too much for us. Worrying about this possibility delayed our departure by another half-hour. Finally we decided to risk everything but, before entering the water, we knelt and offered a short but fervent prayer to God. We asked for help. Misfortunes as prolonged as ours and the constantly renewed calamities to which we had been exposed had made us feel as never before the need for supernatural aid and recourse to God. This duty accomplished, we sprang into the water, committing ourselves to divine Providence, which alone sustained us and saved us from death on the crossing.

The seafloor proved extremely uneven. In fact we were always either climbing or walking downhill and were no more than a hundred yards from the beach when suddenly we were out of our depth. We could not help going under. This mishap disheartened us. We almost decided to retrace our steps. However, by swimming forward we soon found our footing again, and realized that what had so shaken us was no more than a pothole in the seabed, which we would have missed altogether on a line of march ten or twelve yards from it. We completed our passage without accident, wading through water which varied in depth but was never more than chin-high.

Once on dry land again we could go no farther. We threw ourselves down to rest and gather enough strength to continue. Luckily for us the weather was unusually fine. No clouds obscured the sun, whose vertical rays struck us directly, warding off the cold against which, in our situation, we could not have protected ourselves, and drying the clothes and blankets we had brought with us.

After we had rested awhile, we restored our vigor by gathering some shellfish, which chanced to be at hand. A little farther away, we found a kind of well containing drinkable water, which quenched our thirst. Immediately thereafter, we made for the place where the pirogue was supposed to be and soon took possession of it: no one else was likely to dispute its ownership. We inspected it with eager and inquiring eyes. The result was disappointing: its condition was deplorable. On first examination, it seemed impossible ever to make it good for any purpose, but we were unwilling to accept this verdict. After a long and painful trip in the hope of making it sailable, we could not accept, on first sight, that we had been wrong. We looked at it again from every angle, we probed every section of it, and I recognized that all repair efforts would be futile. Desclau and La Couture disagreed, and I yielded to their arguments. After all, there was no danger in trying to make it seaworthy. Only time and labor would be lost. We were used to labor and, as to time, how else could we use it? Working on it, moreover, would occupy us and foster a feeble remnant of hope, all of which was to the good in a situation as bleak as ours.

For our endeavor we had to range far afield. We gathered swags of a certain plant called Spanish moss,[29] which grows in the tops of trees. We intended to use it to caulk our leaky craft. This task used up the rest of the day. We had to stop working early, in order to look for food which, fortunately, proved to be available.

The sun had just set. A biting wind began to blow, threatening us with a very cold night. Whenever we found ourselves in this situation, we bitterly bewailed our inability to light a fire. For us, chancing on the smallest pebble would have been to find the most precious treasure but, as I have said before, we saw none on these islands. At this moment I recalled that the Indian who had behaved so barbarously toward us had changed the flint of his musket on the day on which he had made us halt on this very island. This memory was a ray of brightness which lit a small hope in my soul. I suddenly jumped to my feet, startling my friends. Without telling them where I was going, I left them and ran to the spot nearby where Antonio had disembarked us. There I recognized the place where we had spent the night. Still visible were cinders from the fire we had lit. Slowly I surveyed the surrounding area. I paid particular attention to the place where Antonio had inserted a new flint into his piece and thrown down the used one. There was no corner that I did not inspect scrupulously, and not a blade of grass that I did not lift, to see if it concealed the precious flint. After a full quarter of an hour I was still empty-handed. Night was falling and the last remnant of twilight fading, making it almost impossible to see objects of any sort. I abandoned hope and was dejectedly preparing to rejoin my companions when I felt something beneath one of my bare feet, for I had taken off my useless shoes. Whatever it was under my foot was hard. I stood stock-still, trembling inwardly, torn with both hope and fear. Gently I lowered myself and squeezed my shaking hand below my foot, which I had not dared to move in case I lost the object it covered. I laid hold of it. It was indeed the musket flint I was looking for. I realized it with an ecstasy which it would be difficult to describe, and which would no doubt surprise you or others who have not been in my situation. In this used flint, they would see nothing but a wretched pebble. But oh, my friend, can you still be ignorant of how dire need, and the misfortune which obstructs its fulfillment, lent importance and worth in our eyes to the most ordinary things?

I ran exulting to my companions. "Good news!" I yelled from a distance, even before they could possibly hear me. "I've found it, I've found it!" At the sound of my shouting, they ran toward me, wondering what had happened. I showed them my flint and told them to collect firewood. I pulled out my knife, the only iron object we possessed, and tore off my shirt cuffs to serve as touchwood. I managed to light a huge fire which protected us from the night's cold and which refreshed and warmed our weary limbs. How delightful this night seemed compared to those which had gone before! With what voluptuous pleasure we stretched out around our fire! How long and tranquil our sleep was! Nothing disturbed us until the sun's rays awoke us at daybreak.

I cannot tell you with what care I carried the flint, literally for us a precious stone, which provided us with fire. The fear of being deprived of its comfort through loss of the flint ensured that I took every precaution to protect it. I kept it with me always, wrapped in two handkerchiefs which I tied around my neck. Even so I could not stop myself from interrupting my work every so often to touch it with my fingers to make sure it was still there.

We spent all of our second day on this island in continued efforts to repair the pirogue. We frapped it with one of our blankets which we sacrificed for the purpose, completing the task as the day came to an end. We passed a second night full of hope that our efforts would not be in vain. Eagerness to test the pirogue woke us early. We could not wait to launch it—but everything we had done had failed to make it seaworthy. Entrusting oneself to it was impossible. La Couture still believed that it might be made sailable if we used two more blankets. He suggested that he should take it to the island where we had left his wife and son. Desclau and I, by contrast, thought of looking for a way of getting to the island on which our eight sailors were stranded, finding Antonio, and forcing him to lead us to Apalache or dying in the attempt. We promised La Couture that we would not abandon him if we succeeded but would send him prompt assistance. If we failed in our plan, we would rejoin him. We said goodbye to him and walked to the other end of our island. It was a wasted effort. We could see no passage that it would be prudent or even possible to attempt. A three-mile-wide strait separated us from Antonio's island. Crossing it was out of the question for two men on their own who had only the strength of their arms and legs to assist them.

We retraced our steps. We did not find La Couture on the beach where we had left him. He had already gone in his pirogue to rejoin his wife, no doubt skirting the shore. We went back over the same route we had used in coming to the island. It was not until evening that we reached the channel we had to cross. We decided to delay our attempt until the following day. No doubt our weariness would have precluded success. We remembered the fright we had experienced the first time we had tried it, and did not think it sensible to commit ourselves to a night crossing. Bad luck makes people extremely timid. At certain moments they vainly call on death as a relief and an end to their misfortunes. If it actually draws near, they struggle with all their might to escape it.

The next day we waded back across the channel, with as much ease as on the first occasion but with fewer missteps, and found Madame La Couture. During our absence she had been concerned for our safety. Her husband was with her, having arrived in the pirogue the previous evening. Although he had met with no accident, his short trip had considerably weakened the pirogue. The work we had done on it had given it no permanent sturdiness. Most of its parts had cracked open, making leaks inevitable in many places. At first our failure discouraged us and we put aside the idea of further work on it. We rested for the remainder of the day. The musket flint which I brought back was a blessing for Madame La Couture, who had lacked the comfort of a fire for longer than we, so we lit one which helped restore her strength.

Until this time, oysters and roots had been our only food and sometimes we did not have enough even of these, but Providence provided something different that same day. I had left my companions for a stroll on the beach. Pessimistic thoughts preoccupied me and, unaware of how far I was going, I wandered for a long time. A dead roe-deer which I discovered in my path brought me back to earth. I inspected it from all angles. It was still fairly fresh. It seemed that it had been wounded, and had tried to save itself by swimming to this island, where loss of blood, and the pain which its wound must have given it, had doubtless compelled it to stop, whereafter it must soon have died. I considered it as a present from God and, loading it with some difficulty on my shoulders, I returned to my companions, whom I rejoined after walking for about an hour.

Everyone in our little community was surprised by my lucky find, and thanked God for it. We desperately needed food more substantial than the daily fare on which we had been surviving. We began to prepare the best meal we had enjoyed in a long while. We crowded around our deer, which we had skinned and dismembered, cooked on the fire enough of it to satisfy us, and immediately afterward slept peacefully.

The following day, 26 March I believe, the longing to escape from our island made us turn once more to our pirogue, on which we immediately resumed work with new enthusiasm. We could not have given it up without mortal regret. The poor success of our first repair did not deter us from undertaking a second. We persuaded ourselves that we did better in this second attempt, because we had profited from experience, which had revealed the mistakes we had initially made. We used the same kinds of materials that we had employed before. We did not rush, spending three whole days on the work, to which we sacrificed two more blankets to strengthen the frapping. When our work was done, we had little reason to feel satisfaction. The ramshackle pirogue was in the ocean no more than fifteen minutes before it began to take in water. This failure drove us to despair. We could think of no remedy. Nevertheless, we had to negotiate a mere six miles of water to reach the mainland. For all of us to sail in the pirogue was out of the question. It would have sunk the instant we got into it. Three of us, La Couture, Desclau, and I, decided to make the attempt. While two rowed, the third would bail, using our hats. Thus we seemed to minimize the danger of the voyage. Actually it was as great as ever, but now we had no alternative but to brave it, to look to Providence for the help we needed to complete the crossing safely.

We did not put our plan into operation at once, but deferred departure for twenty-four hours. We spent the rest of the day on which we made our decision persuading Madame La Couture to wait behind on the island with her son and my slave until we could send over a sturdier craft for her, which would be easy, so we told her, once we had reached the mainland. It was not easy to talk her into letting us leave without her. I promised to let her have my flint and my knife. I admit that only with the greatest reluctance did I agree to part with these two items, which had been so useful and which I might need myself, if the pirogue wrecked, for example, or if I arrived in an uninhabited place. It was unthinkable, however, that she should be left with nothing to help her.

Once we had overcome her misgivings, we collected provisions for her. We also gathered some for ourselves, which we put aboard the pirogue. At last, at daybreak on 29 March, we climbed into the frail craft. It was afloat. We felt the bottom of the pirogue on which we were standing bending under our feet. The weight of three bodies as heavy as ours made its seams open a little. Soon we saw water seeping in. This sight drove me to utter despair. I could not suppress an inward shudder. A deep irresistible fear gripped my soul. I foresaw my death. No longer ready to risk the voyage, I suddenly leaped from the pirogue. "No, friends," I cried to La Couture and Desclau. "No, we can't go on with this! We won't do a mile in this thing! Before then we'll be sunk. We'll be at sea, a long way from the shelter of an island. Let's stay on this one. Let's wait for God's help or perhaps for death, but there's no point in bringing forward our hour of dying. When it comes, perhaps soon, let it be welcome as a reward for our patience and resignation, a blessing ending our long torment."

I had waded ashore while declaiming all this. La Couture urged me to get back in the boat, and made fun of my fear. He would not listen to me, and persisted in his intention of staking all on one card; Desclau agreed with him. So they left, and I lingered on the shore watching their progress. I saw them painfully making their way forward, and then rounding a small island[30] which was a musket shot from ours and thus disappear from my sight. I have no doubt that they died. I have never received any news about them. That the pirogue soon foundered is unquestionable. Had the small island not hidden it, I would have seen it sink and watched my unlucky companions go under with it. The unanswerable evidence is the pirogue's rotten condition. Odd reports, which I have since happened to hear, and which I will discuss in due course, merely confirm their fate.

I returned to Madame La Couture, who of course did not expect to see me again. She had not wanted to attend our departure. She had agreed to it with misgivings and seeing us leave would have aggravated her grief. I found her sitting near the fire, her back to the shore and weeping bitterly. My presence revived her. "So you have not left yet?" she said. "What's stopping you? I thought your going was certain so I was trying to get used to being alone. The hope that you would not forget me was my only comfort. Now you're here again. I daren't feel too happy about it. Regrets will soon wipe out my relief and I shall feel worse than before."

I did not think it would be kind to increase her uneasiness by telling her the true reason for my return and of the fear that I felt for our two voyagers of whom one, of course, was her husband. I played down the risk he was running. I simply told her that I had preferred to stay behind in order to lighten the pirogue and that Captain La Couture was relieved by a decision which decreased the perils of his trip. In fact the captain had assured me that he was easier in his mind for having a trusted friend with his wife and son and was less troubled as he set off on his voyage. I further told her that I had promised to spare no effort in helping them to the best of my ability. Madame La Couture replied with obvious gratitude. My presence seemed to console her and to make her quite confident about the future.

Now only four of us were left on our island and it was up to me to take care of the survival and feeding of us all. Madame La Couture and her son were too weak to be of much help and my black was not much better. He was a kind of living machine, who had only the strength of his arms and legs to offer. He lacked judgment and could not look ahead. As I did for the other two, I made decisions and used foresight for him. He was useful to me only when action and the use of his strength were needed.[31]

During the several days that followed, deadly winds from the south and southeast blew continuously. They precluded our finding seafood and we had to subsist on barberries which provided very mediocre, insubstantial nourishment:

they abated our hunger without satisfying it. The roebuck I had found was soon eaten. The good fortune which had presented it to us did not recur and it would have been unreasonable to expect a repetition. Our suffering increased as time passed.

Six days had elapsed since the departure of La Couture and Desclau. At first I hoped, feebly it is true, to have news of or help from them, but soon I dared to nourish hope no more. Madame La Couture herself stopped counting on them. She told me that she had no faith in seeing them again and she had no doubt that they were dead. I could not allay her fears and suspicions. I experienced them myself and I knew better than she the fragility of their boat. The uneasiness I felt combined with prolonged hardships made me bored, disgusted, and ill-tempered. In that state of mind I was incapable of disguising what I thought and of speaking discreetly.

Fed up with my irksome situation, and recognizing that it was up to me to find a way of changing it for the better, I thought of constructing a raft which could take us all from the island.[32] I felt sorry that I had not had this appealing idea before my two companions left. They could have assisted me in the necessary work, which would have had a much better chance of a successful result than the labor we wasted on the wretched pirogue we had traveled so far to find. In any case I decided not to delay in putting the new plan into operation while I still had the strength to go through with it. When I told Madame La Couture about it, she enthusiastically agreed. Overcoming the natural weakness of her sex,[33] which hardships had increased, she threw herself into the work physically. All four of us participated in different ways. I had young La Couture strip the creepers from trees, pointing out the ones which would be most useful. His mother, the black, and I got together the largest logs we could find. Many of them were difficult to move. The three of us combined our efforts to roll them to the beach. Eventually we amassed there twelve good ones but this job alone took us an entire day. Because we were so weak we had to take frequent breaks, but after regaining our breath for a few minutes, we would set to work again. It was only the intense longing to get out of our place of exile which made our persistence possible.

When nightfall forced us to stop work, the three of us were unbelievably weary. We were delighted to find near our fire a large pile of oysters, clams, wing shells and other mollusks. Young La Couture had collected them from the seashore. Eaten raw, these cockles were coarse and indigestible. We thought of grilling them on the fire's embers, the first time it had occurred to us. We tried it with good results. Cooking made this kind of food lose some of its unattractive qualities. It became lighter and more nourishing but it tasted worse. We had nothing to season it with. A little salt would have been enough, but we had none, and did not know how to make it. The raft occupied us completely, leaving no time for culinary experiments. We could survive without salt, but spending our lives on the island was unthinkable.

We resumed work on the raft on the following day. We used the creepers gathered by young La Couture to tie our logs together. I did not think the knots would hold and had Madame La Couture cut one of our blankets into strips, which provided more secure lashings. Meanwhile my black brought me several lighter pieces of wood which I lashed to the logs we had already tied together. My raft was finished at noon. For a mast, I took a length of wood and fastened it, as best I could, in the middle of the raft. I attached a whole blanket to the mast to serve as a sail.

We then unraveled some of our stockings. We used the thread to make shrouds, braces, and sheets.[34] These tasks kept us busy for the rest of the day, but at last we were finished. I added a final branch of medium size, which I intended to use as a rudder. Determined to embark at dawn on the following day, we at once began to lay in a stock of oysters and roots. We were lucky enough to find an unusual number of them, loading as many as we thought necessary onto the raft, which we placed carefully on the sand. The rising tide, which normally came in at daybreak, when we intended to leave, would float it off. While awaiting this happy moment we lay down near our fire. We did not sleep long. A severe thunderstorm blew up during the night. We awoke to rain, flashes of lightning, and the noise of thunder. The sea rose high and the waves went wild. We feared with good reason for the raft which had cost us so much labor. After shattering it, the waves floated its pieces and dragged them out to sea. The dreadful weather lasted all night, ending only at sunrise.

We ran down to the beach to see if any of our creation had survived the storm, but found nothing. Every stick of it had disappeared. Our courage evaporated. We spent the rest of the day glumly complaining, with no thought of trying something new. Then yet one more scourge afflicted us. From the beginning of our ordeal we had suffered no illness. Our health had held up and the only physical inconvenience we had experienced was loss of strength.

While we sat around grieving, my black had run along the coast looking for shellfish. He found none, but did come upon and bring to us the head and hide of a porpoise. Both looked badly decayed, but need drives out fastidiousness and our empty stomachs craved this food, despite its loathsome appearance. We ate all of it. One hour later we all experienced intolerable queasiness. Our stomachs were overburdened and we could not bring up the disgusting offal we had swallowed. We tried water. Fortunately we had plenty and drank deeply, which helped, but only gradually. We were all afflicted by violent dysentery which kept us idle for five days.

The notion of building another raft had been with me ever since the first was carried off, but the lassitude brought on by disappointment made me defer action at the time, and I was in no condition to build one during our time of sickness, which ended at last but left us extraordinarily feeble. The fear of getting even weaker decided me. I would get on with the construction of a new raft. It would not do to wait until my reserves of strength were completely gone and forced me to give up my plan forever. I asked Madame La Couture to help me again and like me, although she did not feel like it, she made the effort. We all set to work except for her son, who was extremely ill. It was then 11 April or thereabouts. We worked unstintingly with as much speed as our depleted strength would allow. Not until the evening of 15 April did we finish. Rolling the trunks that we required gave us the greatest of difficulty. We had to range far and wide to find them. Those nearest to the beach had already been used for the raft we had lost. We fretted constantly that bad weather would interrupt our labors and destroy the raft before it was complete. Preventive measures were impossible. It had to be made on the beach and very close to the water so that, in rising, the sea itself would launch it.[35] To set it in the ocean ourselves was out of the question. We simply lacked the strength to move it. So it was that the smallest cloud in the sky or the slightest increase in the wind's force seemed to presage a storm and alarmed us. At such times we stopped work. We had not the heart to go on with our labor with the thought that, for the second time, it would all be futile.

Eventually we would return to work, worrying and with no enthusiasm. We sacrificed what was left of our blankets and stockings for the second raft. If the waves had carried it away, we would have been left without further resources and without hope. There would have been nothing for us to do except wait for death.

We remained fearful on the night of 15/16 April, only slightly reassured by the cloudless sky. We did not sleep but passed the night in collecting enough provisions in the form of shellfish and roots for two days and in loading them onto the raft. If it was still there on the following day, we would embark. At last day broke with a promise of favorable weather.

I went to wake up young La Couture and tell him it was time to leave. He was the only one of our party who had been too tired to stay up all night. I called him. There was no reply, so I moved closer to shake him awake. His body was as cold as marble, unmoving and apparently unfeeling. For several minutes I was sure he had died, but when I put my hand on his chest I felt heartbeats.

Our fire was almost out. Since we were leaving the island and thought we should need it no more, we had not bothered to feed it. I called to my black to stoke it while I tried to warm the body of the unlucky youth by rubbing his hands, arms, and legs. Just then, from a little distance away arrived Madame La Couture. Nobody can imagine her condition, her grief and her wailing at the sight of her dying son. She fell beside the boy in a deep swoon. I was alarmed. While I was busy trying to revive the lad, I could offer her little help, but I was concerned for her, because she seemed in a state as dire as her son's. Once the black had got the fire blazing, I told him to attend to the lad by slowly stimulating the circulation of his blood. With a little attention, I was able to bring the mother out of her fainting fit and concentrated on comforting her with optimistic words. She did not listen, but eventually her son too regained consciousness. A combination of cold night air and exhaustion had cast him into his trance, from which he would never have emerged had I delayed at all in my attentions.

I was placed in a dreadful predicament. Cast away on a desolate island, lacking all the necessities of life, with two dangerously ill companions, I did not know what medicines to give them and at hand had only oysters, fish, vile roots, and water. And what moment had they chosen to lapse into this critical condition? The very instant when we had planned to leave the island for a place where we might find other men and help. To embark with them on that day was unthinkable: they were too weak. Leaving with them would sentence them to certain death. Leaving without them would be inhuman. The very idea revolted me. I could not do it. Yet to stay with them meant that I was likely never to see the end of my ordeal and to see the waves carry off the raft which had cost me so dear. This thought, which the first misfortune of the sort made more painful, rent my heart and plunged me into despair, from which nothing could move me and which grew worse by the minute. I did not hesitate, however. I did what humanitarianism clearly dictated. I resigned myself to all the evils still in store for me, offering them to God for His consideration, and waited for His judgment.

I ran to unload the provisions we had placed on the raft. My heart ached at the sight of it, as I remembered all the perhaps useless work we had put into it. I thought of putting it in such shape that it would be able to resist the violence of the waves for a long time, provided we did not experience another storm. From it I took the mast, the ropes, and everything I could not hope to replace if they were lost, and relocated them in a safe spot sheltered from the sea. Of most importance was the blanket, which I took to our two invalids who desperately needed it. I spent the rest of the day giving them comfort in any way I could. My hope was that my efforts would not only speed their recovery but also remove the obstacles delaying our departure.

The sole cause of Madame La Couture's illness was her painful concern for her son. I succeeded in lightening it a little. I did not try to fill her with hopes that I did not share: I was convinced that the lad would die. Instead I tried to appeal to her stoicism, encouraging her to accept God's will. I thought it important to prepare her in this way for a blow bound to fall, in my opinion, in the near future. The young fellow was in the sorriest state. He was fully conscious, but so weak that he had to remain lying down. His legs could not support the weight of his body and only with infinite effort could he turn from one side to the other. If he wanted to change position he had to crawl on his stomach, dragging his weight.

I kept vigil over him throughout the night. He never shut his eyes and sometimes talked. He gratefully recognized the trouble I was going to for him and regretted that he was delaying our voyage. I have never heard anything more tender or touching than his words in this vein. He was deeply sensitive, possessing compassion and resolution quite unusual for his years. Toward dawn he began to decline: I thought it was a matter of minutes before he passed away. I had taken the precaution of keeping his mother at some distance from where he lay so that, if he happened to give up the ghost, she would not see it. It is a sight that is invariably awful, even for strangers. It would have been much worse for his mother. I doubt that Madame La Couture could have maintained that courage which I had tried to rouse in her and I wanted at least to spare her the cruel sight of seeing her boy's dying gasp. Knowledge of his death would be slightly less painful if she did not witness it.

At that moment, with effort, the lad managed to speak. "Forgive me the trouble and worry I am giving you. I don't expect that your care will save me. I believe my time to die is close. I shan't leave this island. Even if I live for a few more days I cannot follow you. My legs have become completely useless. I'd be no better off if I made it to the mainland with you. The places where people live are not on the coast so I couldn't get to them. I should then be exposed to the attacks of wild beasts in the forest and to crueler risks than I am now. Do you believe me, Monsieur Viaud?"

After a reflective pause he went on: "Leave! don't wait for me. Don't worry about my death. It can't be long. Take advantage of your raft. Start worrying about losing it. With it would go the only hope you have of saving yourself. Take my mother with you. It would be a comfort to me. As long as she is with you I shall not worry about her. Just leave me as much food as you can gather and I shall eat it while God allows me to live. If you reach a place of safety you will not forget me and I know you have the decency to come back here to rescue me, if I am still alive, or to bury me if I am not. Don't answer me," he added, seeing I was about to interupt him. "What I am asking for is sensible. That the frail hope of my ever being in a fit state to leave with you should condemn you to dying here with me is unacceptable. I want to die alone. As for you, get away! Save my mother! And don't tell her about my condition or the advice I have just given you!"

I was astounded by his words. I did not reply. I could not. A confused medley of ideas crowded my mind but they all suggested that our safety depended on following this advice. Necessity demanded my obedience to it. Rocked by compassion, grief, and doubt, I threw myself at the young man and hugged him. My tears wet his face. I praised his courage and encouraged him to be steadfast without revealing my inmost thoughts, but I no longer told him that I could not accept his advice. He gripped my hand, begging me to think hard about his suggestion.

I left him but continued to ponder his counsel. I admired it and thought with horror that we were all done for if I hesitated to embark on the voyage which he seemed to want. Yet the idea of abandoning him drove me to despair. It would have been possible to place him on the raft and let him share our lot during the crossing to the mainland. But once there, what would I have done? He was virtually paralyzed. Staying on the island was less dangerous for him, because there were no wild animals there. This reflection deflected my will to stay with him. My soul accepted the idea of leaving young La Couture, which, I will admit, began to seem less terrible. The interests of both his mother and myself and our certain death dictated a realization that a need more urgent than that then afflicting us should make me ignore any kind of nicety.

Nevertheless I must say that, amid these reflections, others occurred which somewhat offset the blatant inhumanity of my painful decision. I thought that my journey would be short, that I would soon reach an inhabited place, from which I could take a boatful of men to look for young La Couture, and then bring him to his mother. This was shaky reasoning and even less solid was the prospect of success which it offered, but misery made me see my argument as very sound and sensible.

All the same, for the entire day, I could not bring myself to act. In the evening, young La Couture scolded me for delaying. "If your dawdling on this island could prolong my life," he told me, "I should have nothing to reproach you with, but I feel sure your efforts will be futile. It's possible I shall linger on for a day or two but, in that time, another storm might blow up and rob you of your raft. Then you would like to leave but, of course, it'll be impossible. You'll be sorry you didn't listen to me, and your regrets will be all the more bitter because your delay did me no good. I'll have died in sight of my mother and, while dying, I'll have the awful knowledge that she too was bound to die—and soon. I'll leave her in tears and in despair. This place, which she will never be able to leave, will constantly remind her of me and increase her agony. Getting far away might soothe her. Take advantage of this evening to make preparations. Put the raft in order. Gather your provisions. Leave me some of them, and leave tomorrow at dawn. Don't wake my mother until you are about to embark. She will believe that I am no more, and that you want to spare her the dreadful sight of my body or grave. Don't undeceive her. Just leave and try to comfort her!"

A combination of factors—the youth's dying condition, his coolness in urging me to go, and finally sheer necessity— solidified my resolution. I took the blanket in which he was wrapped, giving him instead the overcoat[36] which I wore over my jacket. In addition I stripped off my waist-

coat which I gave him. I then went to step the mast on
the raft and fastened the blanket to it. Meanwhile my black
went collecting mollusks and, finding an abundance, soon
supplied my cargo. I helped him carry a sufficient pile of
food to young La Couture. We dried a lot of shellfish at
the fire so that it would last longer and put it within his
reach. Spring had arrived, the nights were warmer, and
the fire had become less essential.

For several hours I rested, awaiting the time of departure,
but did not sleep. I talked for a long while with the young
man, who tried constantly to make me feel better about
leaving him, and who committed his mother to my care.
An hour before daybreak he began to decline again and
lost consciousness. I could not revive him. From that moment I considered him as good as dead. Dare I say it? In
his passing away I saw a blessing for him and a comfort
for me. I was able to leave him with a minimum of regret.
Day came and he still breathed, but he said nothing. He
seemed to be suffering the final agony. I did not think he
could live another half-hour. Nevertheless I placed as much
food as possible next to him and filled with water all the
oyster shells we had opened so that he would find nourishment if he managed to summon enough strength to profit
from it. I truly had no hope for him and in performing this
chore I had no doubt that it was useless. Recommending
him to God, I ran to his mother whom I woke with some
difficulty.

"Be brave!" I told her brusquely. "It's God's will that we
leave. Let's obey without wasting time. I'm afraid a delay
might be fatal and we won't be able to do anything about
it."

"Oh my God!" she cried. "My son is dead; I no longer
have a husband; I've lost everything!"

With these words she fell silent and burst into a flood
of tears. I did not bother to dry them. Instead I took her
in my arms and with the help of my black, carried her to
the raft. She did not resist at all. I had feared that she would

insist on seeing her son.[37] This very natural impulse would have been hazardous for her and have delayed our voyage once more to the following day. Her certainty that he had breathed his last meant that she had not even thought of doing so. How could she be of any use to him after his death? She had no need to witness such a sight, which might have deprived her of her vitally necessary remaining strength.

Once we were on the open sea, I felt sure that the young man was no more. In this conviction, while steering our craft I prayed to God on his behalf, at the same time entreating God to be kinder to us.

If my memory is not playing me false, we left on 19 April. We floated toward the mainland without experiencing any accident apart from extreme fatigue. Our trip lasted twelve hours, at the end of which we made land. Our first action was to thank God for our safe arrival. We abandoned our raft but from it removed our food, blanket, and the ropes we had made from our stockings.

We moved inland but found the country impassable. There was swamp almost everywhere. Frustrated and disheartened, we had to recognize that we had not yet shaken off our burden of bad luck and would have to continue to bear it on the mainland.

The sun went down. Weariness and our fear of getting lost during the night in unknown country made us think of looking for a place where we could pass the night with a minimum of discomfort. We chose a mound high enough to keep us dry. On it stood three great trees, whose interlaced leafy branches sheltered us overhead. Naturally I had not forgotten to bring my musket flint from the island. With it I lit a large fire, near which we ate some of our provisions. We expected to enjoy peaceful and badly needed sleep, but, scarcely had we shut our eyes than we heard dreadful roars. Scared out of our wits, we started up. It sounded as though wild beasts surrounded us and were calling to one another. We jumped to our feet, terrified beyond all expression.

Fierce animals seemed to be coming toward us; at least we
thought so from their roaring which, minute by minute,
became both louder and more savage, or so we thought.
My black could not contain his fear. He ran to one of
the trees sheltering us and, leaping at it, climbed up with
incredible swiftness and hid himself in its topmost
branches. Madame La Couture had followed him to the
tree. Pressing her hands together, she begged him to pull
her up after him, so that she might join him in his place
of safety. I shouted to her not to leave the fire, because
wild beasts would avoid it. Simultaneously I fed it with fresh
wood. My appeal was futile. She did not listen but continued, amid tears, to plead with my black, who was deafened
by terror. Although I too could not make myself heard, I
did not dare to run after her to bring her back because
I could not bring myself to leave the safety of the fire.

"Help, Monsieur Viaud! I'm a dead woman!" I could not
resist this appeal. Seizing a stout flaming brand and master-
ing my fear, I ran in her direction. I saw her running with
all her might, pursued by a bear of enormous size, which
halted at the sight of me. I admit that his appearance made
me tremble from head to foot. I moved unsteadily forward,
my brand held before me, and joined Madame La Couture.
I helped her back to our blazing fire. The bear did not follow. I made her look at it to learn the lesson that fire can
be successfully used to keep forest beasts at bay. The sight
of the bear, motionless and gazing at us with glittering eyes,
convinced her that I was right—and she was reassured.

The tree concealing my black was several yards away.
Terror had deprived him of good judgment. He had not
even noticed that there was a much closer tree. Soon I heard
a horrible cry coming from his direction. I looked there and,
thanks to the high flames of the fire I had made, I could
see the bear on his hind legs at the base of the tree where
my wretched slave had sought refuge. It was trying to
climb. I had no idea of what I should do to help the black.
I yelled to him to climb to the very top of the tree and

look for flexible branches that could take his weight but not the bear's. These animals instinctively go, as far as possible, for the stronger limbs and avoid those that will bend beneath their bodies. At the same time I ventured to hurl toward this tree some large blazing brands to frighten the animal and deter him from his obvious intention. I threw several of them with such luck and dexterity that they fell at the foot of the tree, crisscrossing as they lay, and continuing to burn there as fiercely as when in the original fire which, because of the attention I had given it, had turned into a brightly blazing pyre. The light from these torches dazzled the bear. It hurriedly slid down the tree, choosing the side of the trunk farthest from the fire's brightness, and made off.

Any sleep that night was out of the question. It was made impossible by the terror instilled in us by the wild animals, whose grunts and howls never stopped, and even seemed to increase by the minute. I have never heard anything so terrifying or chilling. Several bears came near us, close enough for us to see them by the light of our fire. We also saw tigers[38] who seemed to be of extraordinary size. Perhaps fear accounts for that perception. One of them came toward us in spite of our shouting, but several flaming brands thrown in its direction compelled it to shrink away, not before uttering furious roars, to which other beasts replied.

To guard against a repetition of such visits by other animals which might have come even closer, we arranged blazing brands at some distance from our fire in such a way that they formed almost a complete circle. By forcing animals to keep their distance this precaution kept them out of our sight and thus diminished our terror, but only did so at the expense of our main fire. The wood in it was almost all used up and we were afraid that it would not go on burning until morning. Luckily more of the night had passed than we thought. The roars which had so terrified us grew fewer, more distant, and finally ceased altogether as soon as day broke. At dawn, wild beasts return to their

lairs and do not come out of them until darkness falls. I
used this time to collect more wood for the fire and at once
called for my black. I had considerable trouble in persuading him to come down from the tree where he had been
hidden. He finally slid down, more dead than alive. After
the fatigue and fright of the night, we could not resume
our journey. We badly needed rest but were so deeply disturbed that repose was difficult. We dozed rather than slept
until noon. Then we ate a light meal, using up what was
left of our provisions. Immediately afterward we continued
our journey, walking eastward up the coast with the intention of striking St. Mark's, Apalache, but hoping that on
the way we might meet Indians who would consent to guide
us, to feed us, or even to kill us. For us there were worse
fates. In our state of mind we would have sooner died
quickly than continue as we had been living, experiencing
misfortune upon misfortune, on the brink of death from
either starvation or the fangs of monstrous beasts.

Our failing strength prevented us from covering much
ground. After a march of only an hour and a half we were
glad to stop before we were completely exhausted. Mindful
of the previous evening's terrors, we were determined to
have the energy and time to collect a great pile of wood.
We stacked as much as we could in a location similar to
our previous night's campsite. After I had laid the wood
for our main fire, without lighting it, I made a circle of
twelve smaller ones at evenly spaced intervals around it
at a distance of about twenty yards. Surrounding ourselves
on all sides in this way seemed the surest way to preserve
us from animal attacks. Fear, strong enough for a time to
make us forget hunger, dominated our actions. Eventually,
however, we began to look for things to eat. The land all
around was extremely barren. We could see neither shellfish nor edible roots. Our searching proved useless. We discovered nothing that could be eaten. Luckily we did find
water. It was muddy but sweet and we drank a great deal
of it. It was our only nourishment that evening.

Once night fell, I struck a light and set fire to all our woodpiles. I had not wanted to do it earlier: it would have served no purpose and I was anxious to conserve the wood which I had collected with much labor and make sure it lasted all night. We soon lay down for a few hours of sleep before wild beasts emerged on the plain to trouble us with their snarling. Actually they did not disturb us before midnight, until which time we slept soundly. Our utter weariness prevented us from hearing them sooner, or so I imagine from the frightful noise we could hear as soon as we awoke. One could imagine that every savage monster in the New World had congregated to terrify us with its howls. We identified several different species. For us the most chilling were the roars of the lions which dominated other animal noises. We heard them at no great distance. They seemed to be all around, separated from us only by our bonfires. We were profoundly thankful that we had thrown up this barrier, because not one lion came close enough to be seen. This was just as well since, stunned by their roars which told of large numbers, we could not have stood the sight of them. If we had seen but one, we would have anticipated the arrival of others and probably have died of fright.

Madame La Couture and my black were in a dreadful state. More than once I saw them ready to faint. My terror was certainly as great as theirs; I overcame it sufficiently to talk reassuringly to them. Unfortunately, in trying to inspire courage in them, I lost my own. A cold sweat trickled down my body. I trembled, and welcomed the heat of the nearby fire.

By driving away the wild beasts, daybreak ended the terror which had again temporarily overruled our hunger; it returned in full force as soon as our fear abated. So it was that, instead of fear, we endured the cruelest of pangs. To feel ravenous without the least possibility of eating food is intolerable. We tried to satisfy ourselves with everything in sight, gathering anything that might be edible from the ground and putting it in our mouths, but soon spitting it out.

Unlike the previous evening, we gave no thought to rest that morning. We walked on, hoping to find something to eat. We tasted every plant that grew in this wasteland: various types of heather and leafless brambles whose hard stalks were difficult to chew and almost impossible to swallow. The poor success of every experiment increased our despair, even bringing tears to our eyes. At one in the afternoon we halted, utterly depressed and physically exhausted. We lay down on the ground, unsure that we would have the strength ever to get up again. We awaited death, actually begging for it aloud. We could find no hope in looking elsewhere.

Although he was as weak as we, my black, energized by hunger pangs, jumped up and ran to a tree with low branches which his outstretched arms could reach. He tore off some leaves, gobbling them with such amazing eagerness that we thought that they must taste delicious. The notion that here was food made them attractive and we hurried after him to share his wretched meal. Our imagination endowed the leaves with a flavor they simply did not possess. We did not eat them so much as gulp them down. We filled our stomachs without satisfying them. After swallowing a large number, we reflected that eating them to capacity might be harmful and disciplined ourselves to be moderate.

Satisfied with this supposedly nourishing meal, we concentrated on preparing ourselves to pass the night safely. We all rallied our strength to build fires as we had done the previous evening, a task made easy by the abundance of dry wood surrounding us. It was soon finished and we sat down to wait for the proper time to light them, but scarcely an hour after stopping work, we all felt very ill. The leaves we had eaten produced a searing pain in our stomachs. We felt the need for water and painfully dragged ourselves with difficulty to a nearby spring. No sooner had we drunk than we felt bloated. The leaves apparently acted like sponges. We endured fits of retching which gradually relieved us but only to the accompaniment of excruciating convulsions and the vomiting of a great deal of blood.

For a long time we remained by the spring, enfeebled and almost motionless. We truly believed that, incapable of leaving, we were living our final hours. The setting sun saw us in this desperate plight. Night was coming on and we could by then no longer move at all. We bewailed our inability to return to our fires and light them. We already foresaw animals descending on and devouring us. This vision intensified our paralysis. We sighed, we wept, we uttered groans, but lacked the strength to shout.

The descent of true night seemed to aggravate our predicament. Again we tried to drag ourselves toward our fires, exerting our last resources of strength in the attempt, shuddering when we encountered obstacles. At last we reached them, completely worn out. I had scarcely the strength to strike sparks with my flint. With difficulty I succeeded in dropping them on a ruffle which Madame La Couture had torn from her chemise and when, at length, it was alight, I found myself almost despairing of spreading the flame to scraps of dry bark and leaves, since none of us had breath to fan the blaze. This task took us almost half an hour. Finally we were able to throw flaming bark onto our wood, which luckily caught fire without further trouble.

The frightening sounds which we had heard on previous nights began again in the distance. We were thankful we had succeeded in starting a very necessary fire, but for complete confidence we needed to light the others we had set up around us. To this end we made fresh efforts, sharing the chore. Taking two burning brands in each hand, each of us threw them on different woodpiles and then came back for more to start the other fires. Fear lent us the necessary strength and vigor. We took even less time in this operation than our feebleness would seem to have made possible. Scarcely had we finished than the snarls, which we had heard getting near, backed a little way in all directions.

Having successfully started our fires, we sheltered in the protection they gave and were surprisingly happy. We felt rather more secure, because that evening we had lit many more of them, but that did not prevent us from later feeling the sharpest terror. It was made worse by weakness and a need for food. What we had consumed had merely enfeebled us more than before; the effect of eating it had been horribly wearing. Toward the end of the night, however, we slept, undoubtedly from sheer exhaustion.

We did not wake until the day was well advanced, feeling certainly a little better and partially rested, but sharply tormented by the overwhelming need to eat. We looked with a shudder and deep loathing at the tree whose leaves had seemed so appetizing the previous day, and which had brought us within an inch of death. We got up and continued on our way, hoping to discover at last something better able to sustain us. As on the previous day, we made several experiments with different substances but had as little success. All we found were trees and shrubs which provided nothing.

Our hunger pangs became increasingly sharp. Only the hope of easing them directed our steps and kept us walking until noon. Our gaze wandered all around us, even scanning the far distance, but discovered nothing promising. We stood on a ridge. On all sides we saw a boundless skyline. On our right was the sea and our left a forest stretching as far as the eye could see. In front of us, in the direction in which we had determined to go, was a dry empty plain on which could be seen only the traces of wild beasts and nothing which could sustain us. This sight threw us into bitter despair. Our battered spirits lost all remnants of courage. We abandoned our originally intended route because we could not see how it could end well and because it contained no promise of comfort or nourishment. Instead we walked downhill to the left, directing our steps toward the nearby forest. It was frighteningly dense. The trees were oppressively close to each other; in some places we could not pass between them. The path we had wanted to follow petered out after a few yards. We found alternative tracks which often doubled back to where we had begun. Others would have taken us deep into the woods and left us without a chance of ever getting out, certain of dying from hunger or animal attacks.

None of these trees apparently offered what we needed to survive. Most of them had the same kind of leaves which had made us so sick.

"It's all over," I said to myself, as anguish stabbed me. "It's all over. We must die. We can't go on any more."

Muttering these words, I threw myself on the ground. Madame La Couture lay down next to me. My black placed himself at our feet a little distance from us. Without looking at each other, we all began to weep. Sunk in gloomy thought, we stayed bitterly silent. We understood each other's preoccupations perfectly. They exclusively concerned our frightful situation. We had no need to talk.

The gloomiest ideas occurred to me then. Is there anyone, I asked myself, who has ever seen himself reduced to my extremity? What other man has found himself in a desert, lacking everything, and ready to die of hunger? I then began to recall the adventures of some travelers driven off course by a storm. Adverse winds and dead calms had kept them in unknown waters, and they had used up their stock of provisions without the possibility of replenishing them. I remembered that, having suffered hunger to the point where they were dying of starvation, the only recourse left to those unfortunates was to sacrifice one of their number in order to save the rest of them. Sometimes it was by lot that the choice was made of a victim who, in losing his own life, prolonged his companions' by giving them his corpse to eat.

Dare I confess it to you, my friend? You are going to shudder when reading what remains for me to tell but, believe me, your horror cannot possibly be as great as mine. You will see to what excess despair and starvation can drive us and you will pity me, perhaps, for the suffering which I had endured.

While I was remembering the harrowing experiences of other voyagers, my wandering eyes fell on my black. They lingered there with a kind of greed. "He is dying," I said to myself madly. "A quick death would be a blessing for him. He is dying by inches and all human efforts are powerless to protect him. Why shouldn't his death be made useful to me?"

I will admit that my mind did not reject this possibility. Affected by the weakness of my body, my reason was warped. Starvation undermined me. I felt searing pangs in my innards. The urgent need to appease them completely dominated me. Alternative ways of doing it were out of the question. There was only one, it seemed. My disturbed mind could not reflect and examine coolly. It formed horrible desires and provided me with countless sophisticated arguments to justify them.

"What crime will I be committing?" I muttered. "He is mine. I brought him to serve me. Of what greater service could he ever be?" Madame La Couture had been entertaining murderous ideas similar to mine. She caught my final words. She did not know what train of thought had led up to them and the reasoning which had preceded them but necessity made everything clear. She attracted my attention in a low voice and when I looked her way she pointed both with her eyes and hand in the direction of my black. Her eyes then turned back to me. They had a literally deadly look and she made an even more expressive gesture with her hand—which I fully understood.

To be unleashed it seems that my madness awaited only the approval of a backer. I did not hesitate for a second. Delighted to see that she thought as I did, I felt justified. I started up and, seizing a knobbly stick which I had used to lean on during our marches, I went up to my black. He was dozing. I brought him out of his stupor by bringing the stick down with stunning force on his head. My hand trembled and I did not dare to hit him again. My heart palpitated. My latent humanity screamed an appeal, depriving me of the strength to go on.

On coming round, the black rose to his knees, clasped his hands together and, looking at me with anguish, said beseechingly and sadly, "What are you doing, master? What have I done to you? Won't you at least spare my life?"

I could not help softening. I wept and for two minutes I could not reply. I could not do anything. At last my hunger pangs overcame the voice of reason. A mournful shout and another signal from the eye of my female friend re-equipped me once more with frenzied resolution.

Beside myself, distraught, affected by an unprecedented delirium, I hurled myself at the wretched black and threw him to the ground. I yelled aloud, both to numb myself and so that I would not hear the black's screaming, which might have blunted my cruel determination. I tied his hands behind his back. I called for my companion, who came to my help in this savage procedure. She knelt on the head of my poor black, while I drew my knife and, with all my strength, sank it in his throat and widened the wound.[39] He died at once.

There was a fallen tree near us. I dragged the black to it and hung him on it head down, so that his blood could drain out. Madame La Couture helped me.

This horrible act had exhausted both our strength and our determination. Our fearful eyes lingered on the bleeding body which, a moment before, had been a living being. We shuddered at what we had just done. We quickly ran to a nearby spring to wash our bloodstained hands, which we could not look at except with horror. We fell to our knees to ask God's forgiveness for the inhuman crime we had just committed. We also prayed for the poor wretch whose throat we had just cut.

Nature manages to combine extremes. Completely opposite feelings gripped us at almost the same time. Although devout sentiment followed on the heels of savagery, it was the latter that soon regained the upper hand. Urgent hunger pangs interfered with our prayers. "Lord," we exclaimed, "you know our situation, our overwhelming wretchedness which pushed us into committing murder! Pardon us in our misfortune and at least bless the vile food we are going to eat. Make it nourish us. We have already paid enough for it."

With these words we got up, lit a great fire, and carried out our monstrous determination. I scarcely dare record the details: the very memory of them turns my stomach. No, my friend, except for this period of my life I have never been a barbarian. I was not born for it. You know me well and I have no need to apologize to you, but you must be the only reader of these words. I would suppress this part of my narrative if I imagined that there would ever be other readers. What an idea they would have of my character! Of what other atrocities would they not suspect me capable? Only by reasoning that, thanks to severe hardships, my sense of right had deserted me might they, perhaps, claim that they understood my actions. Few, however, would be fair enough to ponder my misfortunes and to realize that horrors of the kind which I endured actually effect radical changes in a man's character and that the deviations into which they may lead him should not be classed as crimes.

As soon as our fire was ready, I immediately cut off the black's head. I impaled it on the end of a stick and set it up in front of the blaze. Although I took care to turn it frequently so that it would be thoroughly cooked, our raging hunger did not allow us to wait until it was properly roasted.[40] We ate it quickly and, once we were full, made arrangements to pass the night where we were and to protect ourselves from attacks by animals. We rightly expected that the noise of their approach would prevent us from sleeping and therefore spent the night in dismembering the corpse of our black. We cut his flesh into suitable pieces for grilling on the embers or held them in smoke in the hope of preserving them from decay. We had already suffered appallingly from hunger. The only insurance against it was to secure provisions which would not spoil. We stayed in the same place all the next day and the following night, hoarding our food, eating only what would be difficult to preserve and which, consequently, we would be unable to take with us. We parceled the rest, wrapping it in our remaining handkerchiefs and in swatches of cloth from our garments. We hung these packages from our bodies with the makeshift ropes from our raft.

On 24 April or thereabouts we resumed our journey. The break we had taken had rested us and the food we had eaten had restored our strength. Certain of a supply for some time, we did not fear to move onto the plain which had seemed so frightening on the day when we killed the black. We walked slowly and, now just the two of us, did not set out without remorse for the companion who had previously followed us and whose grisly remains we now carried about us. For several days we walked, enduring great strain and meeting many difficulties. Crossing through canebrakes near the sea or in the middle of bramble patches or thorn bushes and other equally hostile plants, we bloodied our feet and legs.

This annoyance, though less serious than hunger, frequently delayed us. The bites of gnats, mosquitoes, and a host of other insects which we met on the coast so disfigured us that we became quite unrecognizable. The bites covered our faces, hands, and legs, causing them to swell monstrously. In an attempt to avoid them, if possible, we made for the seashore, deciding to follow it thereafter, in the hope too of lucky finds in the shape of edibles to supplement the provisions we carried. We were not mistaken in this expectation. When the tide was out and the weather fine, we sometimes found on the beach small mollusks and little flat fish which we speared with a sharpened stick. All the same we happened on them very seldom and there were never enough to fill us. They were, however, not to be despised and we gratefully accepted them as a gift from God with deep emotion.

I cannot give you the details, day by day, of the painful and apparently endless odyssey which we doggedly pursued. The canebrakes, with which the shore was covered in many places, and through which we were forced to travel, were as wicked as the brambles which we had wanted to avoid. Dry canes, splintered by the wind, tore at our legs, cutting them most cruelly. Wild beasts scared us every night, and even more frightening was the frequent need to prepare and eat loathsome meals. Our murderous madness had receded along with our hunger. Reason had resumed control of our minds and reason recoiled at the very idea of cannibalism. We resorted to it only at times of extreme need, when we had managed to find absolutely no other food and when reborn hunger overcame disgust.

One evening, as we made our customary halt, I felt so weak that I could scarcely summon the strength to collect the wood needed for our fire. It proved beyond my power to build it in stacks around our camping place as I always did at night. My monstrously swollen legs could no longer support me. Luckily it then occurred to me that I could do the job better by burning the canes and briars in our vicinity and letting the wind spread the blaze. Not only would it keep wild animals away, but it would have the additional advantage of easing our journey. It would burn all those awkward canes off our intended path and we would be able to walk more conveniently along the shore by following the fire's traces. We found, the following day, that the fire had literally blazed our route for us. I regretted that I had not thought sooner of this expedient to save us from the leg wounds which gave great discomfort and compelled us to cover only short distances daily.

As a bonus we found lying in our path very appetizing food: two rattlesnakes. One had fourteen joints; the other twenty-one. Thus we at once knew their age, if it is true that they grow an extra ring at the end of each year. The snakes were very fat. The fire had surprised them while they slept and its smoke had choked them. They provided us with fresh meat all that day and the one that followed. We also dried part of their flesh for later consumption and added it to our stock of provisions.

During our journey I found yet another means of increasing our store of food. One morning I spotted a sleeping alligator in a nearby pool. I went toward it for a closer look. The beast did not frighten me, although I knew how dangerous it was. The only idea in my mind was how great an addition to our rations the alligator would make, if only I could kill it. For a moment I hesitated to attack it, not because of fear, but simply from uncertainty as to the best way of killing it.

I went forward armed with my stick, which was of a hard and heavy wood. With it I struck the beast sharply on the head three times with such force that I made it capable neither of attacking nor retreating. It merely opened its frightful maw, into which I promptly sank the end of my stick which was fairly well pointed. I probed for and transfixed his throat and pushing downwards at once to the full length of my arm, I pinned the monster to the ground. He leapt and moved in such a frantic fashion that, if my stick had not been firmly and deeply driven into the sand, it would have been impossible to hold the fierce beast, and I would have become the victim of my daring.

Simply keeping the alligator where he was took all my strength. I was fixed in an awkward posture which prevented me from adjusting my stance to improve my chances of killing the monster. I shouted for Madame La Couture, begging her to come and help. She did not dare to assist directly. She did, however, look for and bring me a piece of wood three or four feet in length. I used it to stun the alligator, wielding it with one of my hands, while I continued to grip the stick with which I had impaled it in the other, until the beast had all but ceased to thrash about.

My companion, bolder now, took my place, enabling me to use both my hands, thanks to which I managed to crush the alligator's head and to cut off its tail.

My victory had taken a great deal out of me: I was shattered, and we did not even consider continuing our journey on that day. We used our time to cook a good meal and to preserve the flesh of the alligator as we had that of our black.[41] We cut it up into pieces about the size of a man's hand. That way they would dry out more easily and we should avoid unnecessary delay. I used the hide to make moccasins for Madame La Couture and myself. We contrived leggings for ourselves from other strips of skin. By wrapping them around our legs we protected them from the bites of the insects which had plagued us: naturally their stings could not penetrate alligator hide. Other strips of hide covered our hands and faces. We used it too for makeshift masks. At first we found them awkward, but by preserving us from insect bites they were worthwhile.

Such were the various types of relief which we derived from our alligator. We spent all that day and the following night in these preparations. Wakeful, we put off until the night after that the need to snatch some rest. We did not want to prolong our trip with breaks. It was already made long enough by the unavoidable brevity of our daily marches.

The next day our progress was thwarted after a mere hour by a river which flowed into the sea. Although not very wide, its current was very swift.[42] I reconnoitered. Hoping to find it fordable, I undressed and waded in to test its depth. I met insuperable obstacles: first the water's depth, which made swimming unavoidable, and second, the strength of the current, which was impossible to overcome and would certainly have swept me into the ocean. Alone I might have been able to cope but Madame La Couture could never have done so. Unbearably frustrated, I returned to the riverbank. We had no choice but to walk inland, following the bank until we found either a more peaceful stretch of river or a place where a shallower bed would make fording feasible.

And so we resumed walking. Two whole days elapsed and we found nothing to inspire optimism. The farther we went, the less practicable seemed a river crossing. Our concern and desperation grew. We had already given up hope of ever leaving Florida. We chanced on nothing to eat in those two days and consequently survived on alligator meat, leaving the black's flesh as a last resort. We worried that we would exhaust all our provisions before arriving at an inhabited place where we could replenish them.

Frightened by our past experience, doubtful of the future, and uncertain of how long our run of bad luck would last, we spent our time in hoping, complaining, and then despairing. The sight of the river invariably flowing briskly seemed to increase our weariness. The seeming impossibility of ever crossing it and the consequent need to keep walking upstream, without knowing when we would strike a crossing point, robbed us of courage.

At the end of the second day on which we had followed this river, I saw a turtle, which must have weighed ten pounds, and I turned it onto its back with my stick. This new providential source of food, for a while, quelled our complaints, converting them in fact to prayers of thanksgiving. Previously we had seen a plump turkey hen, which regularly came to drink at the river, each morning and evening. It seemed to have its nest somewhere near but we looked for it in vain. The hope of finding wholesome food had caused us to make the most minute search for its eggs, but we had no luck. It was a frustration which added greatly to our ill humor and made us curse our fate.

Discovering the turtle to some extent reconciled us to our destiny. We thought of cooking it and our hearth was ready. You can imagine what a shock it was when I could not find my gun-flint! I emptied all my pockets and then turned them inside out. I undid all our packets of provisions. I rummaged everywhere with the most scrupulous attention.

Madame La Couture helped. We did not find it. Our woe was proportionate to the need we had for the flint and to the help it had afforded us. Never has a loss given more grief to a man. We now thought of the turtle, over which we had gloated, with the utmost indifference. We would have willingly exchanged it for the flint. The loss of half of our provisions would have troubled us less. Without the flint, how could we protect ourselves from the cold and the attacks of wild beasts? How could we cook and preserve our food, or keep ourselves dry?

Madame La Couture's distress equaled mine. I reasoned that we must have lost the flint either in the place where we had slept the previous night or on the path which we had subsequently taken. I felt tired and weak but did not hesitate for a second to retrace my steps to look for it. I suggested to Madame La Couture that she might either come with me or wait for me. She had no real choice. Although she was nervous about staying alone, she lacked the strength to make the journey again. At the same time she longed, no less than I, to recover the treasure we had lost. She made me promise not to abandon her and to return as soon as possible.

It was fortunate that we had covered little ground on the most recent stage of our journey. We had walked for a mere hour and a half, and nightfall was still far off. I retraced our path with the intention of returning before darkness fell, but it proved impossible. I was too feeble to move briskly. Besides, I did not take a single step without looking around for the flint. I hoped that I had lost it on the path and that I would recover it without the need to walk very far, but it proved necessary to go all the way back to the place where we had slept.

I had used up a great deal of time. Night had already fallen when I arrived. I could see almost nothing. I looked about in every place where I could discern footprints. It was a fruitless exercise. I found nothing. I lay on the ground feeling all around with my hands. They had to do duty for my eyes, which darkness had made useless. Tired of wearing myself out without result, I ran to the fire which I had lit the previous night to see if I could find an ember which might enable me to revive it and thus give me the light needed for my search. The fire was utterly dead. I found only cinders without the least glimmer.

Overwhelmed by this latest disappointment, as though I had a right to expect anything else, I remained lying down, giving way to deep depression, despairing of deriving any good from my efforts, unable to rejoin Madame La Couture that night, and not even giving thought to doing so. The notion of going back to her without my flint was unbearable. I decided to wait until morning to resume my search, in the hope that in the end I would find it. I went to throw myself down on the pile of ferns, leaves, and various plants which had been our makeshift bed. I thought that perhaps it was there that I had lost my flint. For a moment I debated with myself whether to wait until the following day before resuming my search. It was clearly the most sensible course. Broad daylight was absolutely necessary. I could not expect to find anything in the dark. My reason was fully persuaded but my mind was too agitated to put up with delay.

I passed my hands repeatedly over every part of the surface of the bed but they encountered nothing. My initial intention had been to stop after doing this and to put off a more thorough search until daylight, but in my impatience I could not resist going on. Fistful by fistful I went through the pile of foliage. After examining each handful I put it down elsewhere. I spent the best part of the night doing this. I was losing hope of recovering my treasure because I had been through and displaced every single plant comprising the bed. I stretched my hands finally onto the earth which the plants had formerly covered. They came to rest on the object of my longing. I snatched it up with a joy equal to the distress which its loss had caused me. Holding it tightly, I took all manner of precautions to avoid losing it in future.

While occupied with these activities I was a little concerned about wild animals. Although they came from far away, I could hear their cries and I worried from time to time both for myself and for my unfortunate companion. She was alone and her fear in the middle of the night must have been acute. I thought of rushing to her side to reassure her, if that was possible, but I admit that fear of a dangerous encounter on the way kept me from doing anything for a long time. It finally struck me that the care we had taken to make fires every night along our route must have persuaded the brutes to keep their distance, causing them to retire to the far corners of the wasteland we were crossing in order to avoid the fires. Actually during this time they had never come near the places where we made camp and we had heard their snarling only from a certain distance— which had done much to minimize our fear. At last I persuaded myself that I was unlikely to meet any beasts and with some qualms set off. Several times I was on the point of stopping to light a fire to give myself reassurance, but did not in fact halt. Fear lent me wings and, despite my weak condition, I got back to Madame La Couture about two hours before daybreak. I could easily have missed her and might have wandered far from the place I had left her, because a combination of darkness and fear prevented me from recognizing the spot. Only a moan, which I heard purely by chance and which made me shudder, told me that I was about to pass her by without her seeing me. She had heard the sound of my footsteps and, in her fright, had thought that a fierce animal was coming toward her. It was she who had moaned. I asked at the top of my voice, "Is that you, Madame?"

"Yes," she replied almost inaudibly. "My God, how you frightened me! With you so far away and so late coming back, you have given me some bad moments! Did you hear that horrible snarling? It's been dinning in my ears. When you didn't return I thought you'd been eaten and it wouldn't be long before I was too!"

"I'm still alive," I shouted, "and now I've found you again! Both of us have been petrified with fear but I've found my flint again! We'll have a fire! We'll be able to rest and have something to eat."

Even while uttering these words I was collecting some bits of dry wood. I struck sparks from my flint. For tinder I used a strip from my shirt, which was quite worn out and almost in rags. For a long time I had been using either it or Madame La Couture's chemise to start fires.

We soon had a great blaze going, on which we cooked part of our turtle. Its flesh was extremely tender and succulent. On cutting it open, we found in its body a quantity of little eggs which we grilled on the embers, thus enjoying a food which was as wholesome as it was refreshing. It did wonders for us. We slept afterwards. This needed rest, which lasted five hours, both comforted and strengthened us.

On waking we discussed the advisability of continuing in the direction we were going. The upper course of the river was visible and quite straight. We looked at it and despaired of finding a suitable crossing point for a long time. We decided to risk a passage where we were, for which I thought of building a raft. Solid materials convenient for the job were at hand. They were six trees, defoliated by time, which had floated downstream. They had come to rest on the riverbank near a gnarled tree, which leaned over the river, but whose roots were still embedded in the shore. I got into the water. Luckily it was shallow at this place and, using creepers, I lashed four of the trees together, making them reasonably fast. As best I could, I attached a long pole to them. It was thicker at one end than at the other and was meant to serve as both oar and rudder.

Once I had finished, we prepared to leave. We stripped

off our clothes, making a bundle of them, which we bound
with natural materials. We took this precaution so that we
could save ourselves more readily if some accident happened. Our clothes would have got in our way if we had
fallen in the water. Wrapping all our clothes in one bundle
would make it easier to retrieve them if I had to go swimming in search of them. The outcome would show how right
we were to take these precautions.

Our conditions made prudish conventions irrelevant.
While we traveled together, we were scarcely aware that
we were of different sexes. I was conscious of my companion's gender only because, like most women, she lacked
muscular strength. She was conscious of mine merely from
observing the firmness and courage with which I tried to
inspire her, and the help which my superior strength enabled me to give her. We were numb to other feelings. Our
exhausted bodies, oblivious of all other considerations,
asked only that we supply them with food.[43]

Our fear of possible accidents was insufficient to make
us part with our provisions as we had done with our clothes.
Losing our garments would have been less calamitous than
losing our food. We organized our food packages in such
a way as to be able to hang them from our bodies. They
would survive with us or we would die with them.

We got onto the raft, which I pushed off from the shore,
steering as best I could with the pole. At first the current
snatched at us with a speed which made me shiver. In an
instant it had borne us more than three hundred yards from
the place where we had embarked. I was afraid that it
would sweep us down to the sea. With the utmost difficulty
I labored to cut across it. Finally I succeeded, but only at
the cost of losing way and riding downstream at a monstrous rate so that I expected to reach the opposite shore
a mile and a half lower than the place from which we had
set out.

With considerable effort, I managed to get more than
halfway over the river. The current then slackened and we

had almost reached the spot where it was most placid. Suddenly the current took our raft sideways onto a tree which was near to us at water level. The movement which I made to avoid it brought disaster. The strain broke the lashings holding our craft together, loosing the lengths of wood of which it was constituted. We fell in the water and would certainly have drowned, had I not seized a branch of the tree with one hand. With the other I simultaneously gripped Madame La Couture's hair at the very instant when she was already sinking, no doubt never to reemerge. She was still conscious and I shouted for her not to grasp me with her arms and legs, the better to hold her up. Where we were, the water was very deep. I made her clamber onto the trunk of the tree while I swam around it. Its other end touched the bank, enabling me to lead her there. She sat on shore while I detached the packages of food hanging from me and placed them at her side. I went back to the river to see if I could retrieve our clothes and soon glimpsed them. They were caught in the branches of the tree, but the river was stirring them. At the moment when I dived in, the current had begun to carry them away. I swam in pursuit and had the good luck to catch up with them. Pushing them in front of me towards the shore, I landed them safely.

My first concern was to take the bundle to Madame La Couture who untied it, wrung the clothes and then spread them out. Meanwhile I prepared a fire to hasten their drying and to cook such pieces of turtle as we still possessed. We had actually lost nothing by being wrecked,[44] and shed no tears over the raft which, having brought us across the river, had served its purpose. We would have abandoned it, whatever happened.

After eating a restoring meal, we dried our provisions, an occupation which kept us busy all day. We spent the night where we were. The next day, rested and refreshed, we resumed our journey. Taking our bearings as well as we could, we tried to keep in the right direction for St.

Mark's, Apalache. We were constantly worried that we had lost our way. On the east side of the river the forests were just as dense, and the briars and canes as unpleasant and dangerous as ever. Our shoes, leggings, and makeshift gloves and masks were unserviceable. Immersion in the river had ruined them. As before, brambles scratched and mosquitoes and flies tormented us: our bodies became enormously swollen from their constant poisonous biting. We found even less food than on the western shore. The remains of our black and our alligator were all we had to eat.

Suffering these hardships, which grew progressively worse, we walked for several days. Our bodies and spirits were both affected. Hope with its consoling fancies no longer lulled us. We were in a deplorable condition and looked more like walking barrels than human beings. We walked laboriously, scarcely able to place one foot before the other and rising only with difficulty after sitting down.

Madame La Couture held out longer than I. As long as I had possessed strength, I had been thrifty with hers, and had taken on all the arduous tasks that arose. Her spirits, moreover, were less depressed than mine, because she had let me do all the worrying. Until then, therefore, I had borne the brunt in all respects, but now came a time when I had to give in to sustained misfortune.

One day I was scarcely able to see because the bites of the insects I have mentioned had caused swelling around my eyes which weakened and almost closed them. Feeling beaten and unable to go on, I threw myself down on the shore under a tree about a hundred yards from the sea. After lying there for an hour, I tried to rise to continue our journey, and found it was beyond my strength to get to my feet.

"It's all over," I said to my companion. "I can't go any farther. This spot will mark the end of my journey, my troubles, and my life. Use your remaining strength to try and reach an inhabited place. Take our provisions with you.

Don't squander them by uselessly waiting here for me. I
see that God does not want me to survive. My utter exhaustion is a sign of it. The courage and strength which He has
allowed you to keep means that He has other plans for you.
Enjoy your blessings and think sometimes of the wretch
who has shared your troubles for such a long time, who
has eased them for you as much as he could, and who
would never have deserted you, if he had been allowed
to travel with you provided he could be useful. Let's surren-
der to cruel necessity which is commanding us with its
harsh laws. Leave! Try to survive and, when you are enjoying abundance again, and becoming forgetful of the priva-
tions we experienced, say sometimes: 'I lost a friend in the
wastes of America.' No doubt you will be with Europeans
again one of these days. You will hear of ships sailing for
France. When you do, please do me a favor, the only one
I want and expect from our friendship. Write to my parents
describing the fate of their unlucky son. Tell them he is no
more and that they can divide among themselves the sorry
remains of his estate. They are to do with it what they think
fit, without worrying that I shall ever come back to reclaim
it. Tell them to pray for and pity me."

Madame La Couture did not reply except with tears. Her
emotion touched me: it is a great consolation for the afflicted to see that they have aroused compassion. She took
my hands and pressed them tenderly. I tried again to persuade her to leave me and to show her that it was necessary, but failed. "No, my friend," she said. "No, I shan't
leave you. I shall give you, as far as I can, the care that
I owe you, like that you gave me for such a long time. Be
brave! Your strength may return. If that hope proves false
I shall still have time enough to be left alone in this vast
wasteland, accompanied only by my fears. If I abandoned
you, I would feel sure every minute that God was going
to send wild beasts to rip me apart as punishment for leaving you at a time when I could have helped you.[45] As to
our provisions, we'll try to make do with them. I'll also see

what there is on the seashore. Any that I find will help restore your health. From now on I am going to begin to look
after you. You can't protect yourself against insects, so take
this!"

With these words, she took off one of her two petticoats.
Using my knife she split it in two. With one piece she covered my legs: the other she placed over my arms and face.
They gave me great relief, providing effective protection
against possible stings. My companion then lit a fire and
went to the beach, from which she returned with a turtle.
I thought that the blood of this creature might prove sooth-
ing if rubbed into my wounds. I tried it and advised Madame La Couture to follow my example. She readily did so,
for her head, neck, and arms were covered with mosquito
bites. We then rested, but my feeling of weakness remained.
I felt so ill that I had no doubt that death was near. A large
turkey-hen, which we then saw, flew back into a copse only
a few yards from us, making us think she had a nest there.
Naturally it inspired us to get hold of her eggs. Madame
La Couture undertook to look for them. I was in no state
to go myself, being totally immobile, and so remained lying
by the fire.

I stayed alone like that for about three hours. The sun
had just set and I was in a kind of stupid torpor, unmoving
and almost without the power to think. I can compare my
condition only to that deep calm one experiences between
sleeping and waking. A frightening numbness pervaded my
heavy limbs. I felt no pain but instead a general malaise
throughout my body. At this moment, I heard shouts, which
dragged me from my lethargy and aroused my attention.
I strained my ears. They seemed to come from the seashore.
I thought they must be from a band of Indians following
the coastline and getting nearer.

"Great God!" I cried. "Does this clamor portend the end
of all my hardships? Have You sent these Indians to my
rescue or are they coming to stamp out the last remaining
flickering spark of my life? Whatever You want, I am ready.

Whether it is to strike or to save me, either will deliver me from my sorrows. I will equally accept whichever it is."

The same shouts were repeated over and over. A ray of hope lightened my heart. I tried to get myself up into a sitting position and succeeded only by dint of atrocious efforts. A doleful thought occurred then to lessen my excitement. Perhaps, I reflected, these men I hear are skirting the coast in a boat. Soon they will have rowed farther on and they won't see me unless they disembark. What will become of me if they don't get out of their boat here? In the predicament I was in, how could I let them know that in this place was a wretch needing rescue?

This idea made me desperate. I tried to shout but my voice was gone. My fear, however, of letting slip the only chance of help which had occurred in a very long while restored a little of my strength. I used it to drag myself on hands and knees as close as possible to the beach. I could distinctly see a large open boat working its way along the coast. It had not yet passed me. Rising to my knees I took my cap in one hand and tried to wave it but was constantly thwarted by my inability to hold myself up. I kept falling on my stomach. I much regretted then that I did not have Madame La Couture with me. She would have been able to go to the beach and run along it shouting for help and would certainly have attracted attention. But she was far away and surely beyond earshot of the shouts of the men in the boat. Otherwise she would have come running.

In her absence I did all that I could to make myself visible. I found a pole nearby. On it I fixed my cap and a scrap of the petticoat which my companion in misfortune had left me. This makeshift flag, wafted in the air, caught the attention of those in charge of the boat. I realized it both from their excited shouts and from an alteration in the course of their craft, which now veered toward the shore. I dug my pole into the sand so that they would not lose sight of my signal and let myself drop onto the sand. I lay at full stretch, worn out with the efforts I had just made, but comforted by the certainty of imminent deliverance. I thanked God for the blessing which He had been pleased to bestow on me.

Looking closely at the boat, I noticed that the men crewing it wore clothes. This observation, which persuaded me that I would be dealing with Europeans, rid my mind of fears which would certainly have troubled me had they been Indians. While awaiting my rescuers I cast my eyes toward the fireside, looking for Madame La Couture. I could not wait to see her so that I could tell her of and share with her our good luck. Without her I could not savor it fully. Her tender concern for me and her determination never to abandon me had confirmed the friendship between us, which had been engendered by our joint experience of misfortune. I could not see her and it took something from the joy of the moment; not much, because her happiness was sure to come. It could be delayed only very briefly. Her return could not be far off because it was getting late: nightfall was very close.

At that moment, the people I had been waiting for arrived. My extreme joy almost killed me. It precipitated a physical reaction so severe that, for several minutes, I could not answer their questions. I could not utter even one word. They gave me a drop of taffia to steady me and I was able to say something of my ordeal. At once they realized the danger of my condition and had the good sense not to make me talk much. I was delighted to see Europeans. I knew from the way they spoke French that it was not their native language, but did not ask their nationality. Actually it was of no importance. It was enough that I was among men who wanted to help me.

I begged them to resume their hailing while searching in the nearby copse, so that Madame La Couture might hear them. Her prolonged absence had begun to worry me but, a moment later, all my fears evaporated. She appeared, running toward me with all her might. She had caught the turkey-hen and had brought its nest too.

"My good friend," I said, "these provisions are most timely. We shall share them with these gentlemen that God has directed to rescue us. Rejoice! Luck has not deserted you and your concern for me has received its reward."

As night had fallen, it was pointless to think of embarking before the following day. Until then I had lost track of most dates, but now I learned that it was 6 May. We all sat around my fire, to which my rescuers carried me, and ate our turkey and its eggs. In addition we had some smoked meat and glasses of taffia. The meal was one of the merriest I had enjoyed since the shipwreck. A happy heart helps physical satisfaction. The newcomers told me they were English. Their leader was an infantry officer in the British Army called Wright.[46] During the meal I told him of some of our adventures. I saw him shake his head several times at mention of the dreadful hardships we had endured. When I talked of the need to which we had been put, of looking to my unfortunate black for the food which all Nature denied us in this wasteland, he wanted to see that horrible meat. Curiosity made him try a piece but he spat it out with an expression of indescribable disgust. He pitied us for having been reduced to eating such loathsome fare.

I noticed in passing that only the officer and one soldier spoke French, but that all the rest had made it plain that they wanted to hear my story. I had to tell it in English. Since I had twice been taken prisoner during the last war,[47] I had had the chance to learn the language. Afterwards it proved a great asset and now it helped me gain the goodwill of my rescuers.

When I had completed my tale I asked Mr. Wright what was the reason, so lucky in its outcome, for our meeting. He replied that he was with a detached garrison at Fort St. Mark, Apalache, commanded by a Mr. Swettenham.[48] Some days previously an Indian had reported that he had found a corpse on the beach. The remnants of its clothing showed that their owner was European. His face and stomach had apparently been devoured by wild animals. On receiving this news, Mr. Swettenham had ordered his interpreter and four soldiers to reconnoiter the coast in an open boat and to pick up any castaways they might find in a condition to profit from their attention. Wright added that his superior had noticed how prolonged stormy weather had been that season, and had suspected that a ship had been wrecked. He thought that she might be one loaded with provisions for his garrison that he was expecting from Pensacola.

I had no doubt that the corpse seen by the Indian, whose report had been responsible for Mr. Wright's mission, was either that of the unlucky M. La Couture or of my partner, M. Desclau.[49] Unquestionably both had drowned. One of them might have disappeared at sea and been eaten by alligators, and the other cast up on the shore. Everything points to it, since I have received, from that day to this, no news of them.

After we had talked on these subjects for a while, we drifted into a sleep which was soon disturbed by a severe thunderstorm. The rain, wind, thunder, and lightning continued without pause for the rest of the night. The Englishmen were much put out, but Madame La Couture and I had, for some time, become used to them. They were still more bearable because of the rescue assured us and which in fact we were already enjoying. Our hardships were less keenly felt because we could see an end to them. Our wounds and general debility caused us less suffering and we even began to see them as temporary inconveniences which would soon pass away with the help of a little rest and care.

Dawn saw the storm subside and, as the sun rose, vanish altogether. We thought only of leaving. I had recovered enough strength to go to the boat without help, if need be, but Mr. Wright would not allow it. He made sure that I was carried there. "I'm glad you feel stronger," he said, "but don't strain yourself. Husband your strength. You'll have the time and the occasion to use it later on."

Madame La Couture walked beside me, looking at me as

we went to the boat, with a radiant and naive exultation. "Now," she said, "was I wrong to oppose you and insist on staying with you? We have both survived and can now enjoy a carefree life without regret."

"You're right," I replied. "I would never have forgiven myself for having pressed you to leave me, if our rescuers had arrived without your being able to benefit."

We got into the boat, where I managed to find some rest. Mr. Wright was looking forward to completing his mission. There remained only one island to visit before returning to St. Mark's, Apalache. He steered for it and we arrived after twelve hours of sailing, thanks to a favorable wind. I recognized the island as that from which Madame La Couture and I had rafted and on which we had left her son. The misfortunes I had endured since our departure had scarcely allowed me to think about him. On returning to the island I of course remembered him and could not help grieving over his fate. Amid my regrets I recalled that the boy had not been quite dead when I had left him. The notion that he might still be alive and that we might be able to help him excited me. Reason uselessly tried to reject the idea as totally impossible. I could not rid myself of the desire to find out how he was.

We continued to scud along with the object of circumnavigating the island. At intervals our soldiers hailed at the top of their voices. No one answered. This silence doused neither my fears nor my secret hopes. It was possible that the unlucky youth could hear our shouts, but was too weak to make his own audible. I remembered my own condition on the beach when the Englishmen had arrived. Young La Couture's, if he had survived, would be even worse. I could control my patience no longer. I had to find out what had happened. I told Mr. Wright of my own experience and of my surmises. He tried to convince me of the pointlessness of that kind of search and certainly it seemed that the only result would be to delay us. However, being a decent fellow, he let himself be swayed. He beached the boat and put a man ashore with orders to find out the condition of young La Couture.

The soldier returned after fifteen minutes to report that he had seen the young man and that he was dead. Mr. Wright was ordering him on board when I badgered him again. "I am sure you will think I'm being awkward," I said, "but I have another favor to beg. That young man meant a great deal to me. Only his firm insistence persuaded his mother and me to leave this island. I owe him some acknowledgment. It can't be much, but I would like to do what I can. Please let me administer the last rites. Just give us time to bury him."

Mr. Wright was a model of politeness and agreeability. He consented to this additional request, ordering everyone to disembark and to carry me to the corpse. We all went, including even Madame La Couture. "My unlucky son has followed his father into the grave," she cried amid sighs. "His mother still lives, but rescue is beginning to seem worthless since I can't share it with him."

When we reached the pitiable youngster we found him lying on his stomach, his face pressed into the earth. His body was burnt red by the sun and already stank. He had been dead a long time, it seemed. Maggots swarmed about his thighs. The hideous and disgusting sight pierced my heart. I prayed, while soldiers dug his grave. When it was finished they came over to fetch the body. Imagine everyone's amazement when we then realized that young La Couture's heart was still beating! Just as one of the soldiers bent to take him by the leg, we saw it jerk back! Immediately we crowded around to give him any assistance we could. He was made to swallow a little rum mixed with water. The same liquid was used to wash the sores on his knees, from which we picked out the many maggots which had perhaps caused them and made them fester.

Madame La Couture was overwhelmed. She could not move. In turn she felt fear and joy, as she saw her son, whom she had thought dead, breathing again, causing her to distrust the evidence of her eyes. "Is this possible?" she cried in a kind of delirium. "In the name of God, don't mislead me. Tell me the truth. Please don't give me false hopes which would make my grief all the harder to bear if they are to be dashed."

Having uttered these words, she ran to her son's side, examined him, and immediately afterward looked up, trying to read in our faces what we thought of his condition. A second later, she turned once more to her son, taking him in her arms and trying to revive him with kisses. We were forced to drag her away because she was obstructing the treatment we were trying to give him. I could do very little. I begged her to sit near me and talked of everything which might calm her down. She only half-listened. Constantly her eyes turned in her son's direction. She would suddenly jump up and I had to call on my feeble reserves of strength to restrain her.

"Wait a moment," I told her. "Let these kind-hearted Englishmen get on with their work. Don't interfere! Your impetuousness may do harm."

"All right," she replied. "I'll do what you say. I'll stay here." A minute later she tried to escape me. I begged her to be patient. I repeated my argument and reminded her that she had promised to stay still.

"That's what I'm doing. I promised to and know I must. But, my dear Viaud, I can't control myself. I would be happy just to see him for a moment, one single moment. Why are you holding me back? You're cruel! Oh, if only you knew what it is to be a mother! Did you ever have a son?" Without waiting for an answer she kept asking new questions, asking me what I thought of our ordeal, if I thought that her son could survive, paying no heed to my replies and continually trying to leave me.

Eventually Mr. Wright came to tell us that young La Couture had recovered his senses. His eyes were open and he was weeping. He had looked at the strangers around him and asked first for his mother and then for me. We hurried to his side and he recognized us. "It's you!" he exclaimed in a faint voice. "Is it possible that you are back again? I haven't seen you for such a long time! Where were you?"

It was not the moment for explanations. We told him that we had come to free him from his misery and urged him to be brave. He and I were both carried to the boat. I had him laid on some borrowed soldiers' coats, covered him with others, and gave myself the duty of looking after him on our voyage. His mother did not leave his side for a second and I had no end of trouble defending him from her endless prattling and wearying caresses.

As it was late in the day, we did not make much progress. We reached the other end of the island and disembarked to spend the night there. Three of the soldiers went hunting and had the luck to shoot three fat geese[50] which provided us with a good supper. The young man was able to eat some and slept throughout the night. The following morning he felt better; that is, he was fully in command of himself. He could not, however, give a complete account of what he had done since we had left him. He could tell us only that he had often been delirious and that when he came to, he felt great thirst and hunger. The water and food we had left him were a great help. He was so weak that, in order to eat, he had to pick it up with his mouth, like a dog. He had no idea of the time that he had spent alone in his plight. He did not realize that we had abandoned him. Instead he thought we had gone searching for and found the help which had saved him. We did not then disillusion him. The way in which he had managed to live as long as he did was incredible. If someone else had told us of it, we would not have believed it. All the facts about it in combination made it unbelievable. We had left the island on 19 April and it was 7 May before we returned: which meant he had hung onto life for nineteen days. Without a miracle how could he have survived so long? Madame La Couture and I saw the hand of God in it. She fell to her knees. "Great Lord," she cried, "You have preserved my son and given him back to me! Now complete Your work! Grant me, in this world, compensation for my suffering but, if You want him with You in the next, if You have shown him to me merely to remove him entirely, either grant me the strength to bear this final blow or let me share death with him."

I prayed too, but I dared to hope that all would be well. We embarked the same day for St. Mark's, Apalache. The winds were very favorable and our voyage was brief and uneventful. My observations convinced me that, without the English, we would never have reached St. Mark's. It was about forty-five miles from the stretch of coast where we had been picked up. How could we have successfully traveled them? How could we have crossed the several very wide rivers which lay athwart our route?[51] Sailing past them, I saw their mouths and could estimate their width, depth, and the speed of their currents. In our feeble condition, we would have found them insuperable obstacles. To find fordable places or stretches where we could cross safely by other means, we would have had to diverge from our path several times, and would have been compelled to wander trackless wastes in our search for them. These detours would have multiplied the number of miles that we had to walk. How many is unsure. The only certainty is that we could never have succeeded and would have died in the attempt.

We reached St. Mark's, Apalache, at seven in the evening on 8 May. Mr. Swettenham welcomed us with great kindness. He began by having me carried to his quarters, and by sending Madame La Couture and her son to those of his detachment's corporal. At the same time he ordered his surgeon[52] to give us all the benefit of his skill. He was even good enough to share his bed with me and to make me take one of his mattresses. In addition he had some sheets taken over to Madame La Couture. He omitted none of the attention we so badly needed in his concern to make us comfortable.

Luck had placed us in the hands of a kindhearted man

and we soon felt the benefits. What would have become
of us if he had been of a more callous type, who might
have thought he had done all that decency required in lift-
ing us off the desolate coast, but who then would have left
to us the business of finding the other kinds of help that
we needed?

The end of our sufferings had at last come about. They
had begun in a shocking way on 16 February 1766, when
our ship was wrecked. They had lasted until 7 May—eighty-
one days. They seemed much more because of the countless
horrible trials which we had survived during that time. Is
there anyone who has had worse luck? It is unsurprising
that such prolonged misfortune had eroded our constitu-
tions. Of course our bodies fought back and were eventually
restored, but for several days our recovery was by no means
certain. We had swollen to enormous size.[53] The surgeon
attending us at first despaired of saving our lives. It was only
by feeding us highly nutritional food in very small quanti-
ties that he succeeded in repairing the effects of vile and
insufficient food. Young La Couture's condition was of
course the most dangerous. The surgeon had much less difficulty in healing his mother, but in the end he cured us all.

I stayed in the fort for thirteen days. From an Indian chief
who brought letters to Mr. Swettenham from the English
commandant at Pensacola, I obtained news at that time of
the treacherous Antonio and the sailors who had remained
behind on the island to which he had carried us all. After
waiting in vain for the Indian's return, these wretches had
massacred his mother, sister, and nephew while they were
asleep. They had then possessed themselves of their firearms, gunpowder, and a small pirogue. Since this craft could
hold only five persons, they had cast lots to decide who
should travel in it and who should remain on shore. Thus
three sailors had to stay and wait for a change of luck. With
heavy hearts they watched their companions embark. Two
days later, Antonio returned to pick up the rest of our belongings and take them to his home. He took his revenge

for the death of his kinsfolk by shooting the sailors one after the other with his musket. On returning to his village he boasted of this exploit, thus bringing it to the ears of the Indian chief who told me about it. I have never been able to discover what happened to the five sailors who had set off in the pirogue. Everything leads me to believe that of the sixteen people with whom I had embarked on this deadly voyage only two and myself had survived.

After spending about thirteen days at St. Mark's Fort, Apalache, I found my health improved. My restoration needed nothing except the last touches, so I decided to leave the fort. A chance to do so occurred and I decided to take it, fearing that I might not have a similar opportunity for some time. Vessels seldom came to St. Mark's. One could be there six whole months without seeing one. I had been told that a boat was supposed to leave for St. Augustine on 21 May. I decided to be on it. I thought that I could obtain the medical assistance I needed more conveniently in St. Augustine than in a remote outpost like St. Mark's, where, besides, I could not stay for long without harmfully using up the commandant's stores and his garrison's rations.

Madame La Couture would willingly have come with me, but her son was as yet in no state to make the voyage, and she did not want to expose him to it. She preferred to go back to her native Louisiana, where her family still lived. She had been told that a ship for Louisiana would be available at the end of the following month, by which time her son would be able to take a sea trip without danger. We both parted with regret. The habit of wandering and suffering together had cemented a tender friendship between us. It seemed that something would be missing when we could see each other no more, but we were used to bowing to necessity, which now pulled us in different directions. What made it bearable was that our trials were over and that we had no need to worry about each other's future.

Our farewells were moving. We could not hold back our tears. We promised never to forget each other. Her son, who was in bed at the time, got up, joined us, and, getting to his knees, prayed aloud: "O God, look after this man who has saved my mother, and also returned me to the land of the living. Reward him for these deeds and please discharge my debt to him."

This plea from a decent and sensitive soul touched me more than ever. I clasped him with emotion and said that I was already more than repaid by his words; that he owed me nothing and that, although I had the privilege of being useful to his mother, her help had been just as vital to me. As for him, I had simply done my duty and, by contributing to his removal from the island, I had done nothing but atone for my callousness in leaving him there. Every time I thought of the condition he was in when I found him, I loathed myself. I congratulated myself on my ideas of first searching for him on the ground and then of burying him. I shuddered when I reflected that he would have perished, had we continued on our way after the soldier had come back to the boat reporting that he was already dead.

At length I left Madame La Couture and went to give my thanks and to say farewell to Mr. Swettenham and Mr. Wright. They wanted to hear no words of thanks but embraced me in such a way as to deepen my gratitude. They came with me to the vessel, where I saw that they had already placed all the provisions I needed for the voyage. Both made a point of recommending me to the ship's captain, extracting a promise that he would give me the best of care and provide every service within and even beyond his duty. They embraced me again. Mr. Swettenham then gave me a packet for the governor at St. Augustine and also a certificate describing the situation in which Mr. Wright had found Madame La Couture and me and afterwards her son. At last the two officers left, leaving me full of admiration and gratitude for their conduct.

My voyage from St. Mark's, Apalache, to St. Augustine lasted twenty-four days. I shall not go into its details. Suffice to say that the first thing that the vessel's master did was to forget everything Mr. Swettenham had urged on him. His treatment of me was extremely brutal. I had no right to expect it and I have never known what prompted it.[54] In any case it made my voyage profoundly unpleasant and seem intolerably long. I had the misfortune, moreover, to have no water of my own and the callous captain would give me none. This denial of a liquid so necessary to an invalid almost precipitated a highly dangerous relapse, and without question I should have become seriously ill if we had not been nearing the end of our voyage.

On 13 June I arrived at St. Augustine. The vessel grounded on the harbor bar. The pilot's boat took me ashore, where a corporal met me. He took me to the quarters of Mr. Grant, who commanded in St. Augustine,[55] to whom I handed the packet entrusted to me by Mr. Swettenham. I had reason to praise that officer but I received just as many kindnesses from Mr. Grant. He was loath to let me out of the castle.[56] He arranged for me to have a room and a good bed there. On his instructions, his surgeon attended me. As a result of being deprived of water, I was suffering from throat ulcers and parts of my body had begun to swell again. The care I received in St. Augustine eventually brought the disappearance of all these symptoms. By 7 July I was able to go out and walk around the town. Mr. Wright and Mr. Swettenham had saved my life and Mr. Grant's generosity enabled me to keep it. I cannot think without emotion of the kindness which all three showered on me. I was an unknown foreigner who hardly had any right to expect it, but I was down on my luck and that was enough to arouse their benevolent concern.

I lived in the castle with Mr. Grant[57] until 21 July, when I left for New York. I shall never forget the way in which the generous governor crowned his kindness. He was good-natured enough to summon the sloop's captain, and to recommend me, giving him thirty-seven shillings for my passage. Then, having himself chosen the basic rations I would need for my voyage, he added some particular delicacies and had them all put on board. He thus provided luxuries as well as what was necessary. Moreover he supplied me with a small chest full of linen and garments which I badly needed. I then went to bid him goodbye and thank him. "Let's not talk about that," he replied. "You were in distress. I did only what I would want someone to do for me, if I ever found myself in a situation like yours. All the same I have not done enough. You must be penniless and you will need money. You will find employment in New York but I doubt if you will find it waiting for you immediately on arrival. It could be that several days will pass, during which you will, of course, have needs to pay for. Perhaps these ten guineas will tide you over. I hope they will be enough."

Mr. Grant pressed the coins into my hand. His fore-thought in giving them to me, combined with his previous generosity, affected me greatly. I tried to stammer my thanks but emotion overwhelmed me. Deep feeling is always difficult to express. Mr. Grant embraced me. "It's a trifle," he said, "and you are too sensitive. You'll embarrass me if you talk about it. Do as I do—forget it. Already I can remember nothing about it." I was compelled to keep my mouth shut but my heart and eyes expressed my feelings. At that moment someone arrived to say that, but for me, everyone was ready to sail. So I most regretfully parted from my benefactor. After a voyage of fourteen days under the command of a captain much more humane than the other, who would have paid as much attention to me and shown me as much consideration, even if I had not been recommended to him, I arrived in New York. It was 3 August. I made myself known to the French community in the city. Touched by my plight, they gave me every assistance and introduced me on 7 August to Monsieur De Peyster, one of the city's richest merchants, who at once generously offered me a job. However, after he had heard the tale of my unprecedented ordeal, he told me that it would not be sensible for me to think of working for some time. "After what you have suffered," he said, "you need a long rest. To restore your health you should be free of all worry about the present or the future. You also need care and medical treatment. Leave all that to me. From now on you will be my guest. In my house you will have a good room, a good bed, and plenty of healthy food. Once I have seen that you are completely recovered, I shan't prevent you from looking for a job. In fact I'll give you one myself. Do these arrangements suit you?" he asked as he took my hand. At once he gave orders that my apartment should be made ready and that I should have everything I needed.

I shall say nothing of the gratitude that I felt. Ever since I had been found dying on the desolate Florida coast, I had met only humane, sensitive, and generous souls. Are there many like that? They have compensated me for my misfortunes, but for which I would not have met those kind people.

While I dwelt peacefully at M. De Peyster's, I wrote to my family telling them that I was still alive and that I had undergone inexpressible hardships for eighty-one days. That is the letter that you have been shown and which, as my friend, you found too summary. I sent it by a vessel sailing for London, at a time when I did not know how long I would be staying in New York. I expected no reply until I knew my eventual destination and could supply a firm address.

M. De Peyster lodged me in his home until February 1767, when he suggested that I take the snow[58] *Le Comte d'Estaing* to Nantes. As a result I sailed on 6 February, arriving safely on the twenty-seventh of the same month. My snow was destined for a Mr. Walsh whom I found as responsive to my misfortunes as his business associate, M. De Peyster. At Nantes I wrote again to my family and it was there that I received their replies and your letter. You asked for a detailed account of my adventures. Being unable to refuse anything to a friend, I have used such spare time as my business has allowed me to put them down on paper. I am sure that my sad tale will move you and arouse your pity for me. Perhaps the promptness with which I have rushed to grant your wish will further convince you of the firmness of the lifelong attachment to you to which I have committed myself and of the importance which I attach to your reciprocating it.

Certificate given by Mr. Swettenham, officer commanding St. Mark's Fort, Apalache, to M. P. Viaud, ship's captain.

I, the undersigned George Swettenham, lieutenant in the British Army, of the 9th regiment of foot and officer commanding St. Mark's Fort, Apalache, certify that, on intelligence from an Indian who told me that he had seen a dead body on a beach about forty miles from St. Mark's Fort, having good reason to believe that some vessel had foundered in nearby waters and fearing that she was one which I had been expecting for several days of which I had received no news, I detached four soldiers and my interpreter under the command of Mr. Wright, ensign in the same regiment, to reconnoiter the coast and give help to any distressed people who might have been shipwrecked on it. On his return Mr. Wright introduced me to M. Viaud, a Frenchman, and a lady whom he had found on an uninhabited part of the shore. Both were in a desperate condition and almost dead from hunger, since they had eaten nothing but a few oysters and the remains of a black whom they had killed in order to survive themselves. M. Viaud has told me that he was a captain in the mercantile marine, and a reserve officer in the king's navy. He alleged that an Indian that he met who had promised to lead him here to St. Mark's had stolen from him everything that he had salvaged from the shipwreck, and then made off in the night in his pirogue, leaving Viaud on an uninhabited island. Mr. Wright also brought back a young man, son of the lady who accompanied M. Viaud. He had found him on an island in a sad state. It seems certain that, if he had not been rescued, he could not have lasted another twelve hours without food. When found he had lost consciousness and all ability to move. The shocking situation in which they were found, their extreme weakness and what I have since learnt from some Indians, all persuade me that M. Viaud's account on the subject of the Indian who robbed and abandoned him is true. In this belief I have given this certificate to M. Viaud who is bound, once he is able, for St. Augustine, to proceed from there to some French colony.

Translator's Notes

1. Probably indigo, Louisiana's main export in the 1760s, but possibly tobacco.

2. The consequences of acting on this misidentification could have been fatal. Rounding Cape San Antonio and sailing north would have brought *Le Tigre* into the open waters of the Gulf of Mexico, but rounding the Isla de Pinos and sailing north would have taken the vessel onto the shoals and rocks off Cuba's southern shore.

3. Antonio de Ulloa was the first Spanish governor of Louisiana. He had left Havana to assume his post in the frigate *Volante* on 17 January 1766 but, because of the same bad weather that beset Viaud, did not arrive in New Orleans until the last week of February. See John Preston Moore, *Revolt in Louisiana: The Spanish Occupation, 1766–1770* (Baton Rouge: Louisiana State University Press, 1976), p. 20.

4. A necklace of islets curving from north to south between the coast of what is now the state of Mississippi and the mouth of the Mississippi River.

5. They probably knew that there was a fort and trading post at Apalache.

6. A musket shot was 300 yards. See John Creswell, *British Admirals of the Eighteenth Century: Tactics in Battle* (New York: Archon, 1972), p. 93.

7. Frapping (Fr. *cintrer*) is the practice of securing a vessel by passing turns of a cable around the hull at its center to strengthen it.

8. An English fathom measures six feet, but a French fathom, such as that to which Viaud was accustomed, measured just under four feet, four inches.

9. The counter (Fr. *arcasse*) was the arch forming the

overhanging stern of a vessel above the waterline. Presumably breaking it off with bare hands, normally out of the question, was possible for Viaud because natural forces had already torn off the rudder and probably the transom too (p. 43).

10. That Viaud and his companions found oysters then and later is surprising. Although the Apalachicola area abounds in oysters they are today found only on the mainland side of the waters where Viaud was wrecked, not near the islands. That Viaud, a seafarer brought up on the west coast of France, might have mistaken other kinds of mollusks for oysters is unlikely.

11. In the eighteenth century ship's biscuit meant flat cakes of dense, hard bread which had been mixed with the least possible amount of water and slowly baked. Since it was not cooked aboard ship it was sometimes months or even years before it was eaten, by which time it was often infested with red or black weevils.

12. Viaud used the phrase *mouchoirs de pariaca*. *Pariaca* does not appear in any standard dictionary. Griffith translated *pariaca* as "Indian silk."

13. As supplies for the castaways, Viaud's find was scanty. In navies of the day the standard daily ration for each man included one-and-a-half pounds of biscuit.

14. Since matches in the modern sense had not yet been invented, and Viaud did not mention finding a tinderbox, they probably used a flint from one of the muskets Viaud had retrieved to light the fire.

15. In fact rum, not brandy, was the drink most commonly traded.

16. White rum.

17. Destroying the rum seems needlessly rash. The liquor was obviously drinkable by itself and was certainly useful in making brackish water potable. Perhaps, with the safety of Madame La Couture in mind, it was the sailors rather than Indians that Viaud wanted sober, although destroying the barrels was not his but a collective decision, according

to his account. The reasoning behind it is unfathomable. If three barrels could be buried, why not all?

18. It is plausible that the Indian should have a Spanish name and speak some Spanish if his home was St. Mark's, Apalache, for it had been an outpost of Spanish Florida for many years before a British garrison took over on 20 February 1764. See Charles L. Mowat, *East Florida as a British Province, 1763–1784* (Berkeley and Los Angeles: University of California Press, 1943), p. 10.

19. Probably part of what is now St. George Island, west of Dog Island, is meant.

20. In fact Antonio's estimate was not far off. From the eastern end of Dog Island to St. Mark's is thirty-two miles, and from the eastern end of St. George Island, forty-one. Viaud himself would later say (p. 117) that the distance from the point where he was ultimately rescued to St. Mark's was forty-five miles.

21. William Falconer's *Marine Dictionary* (London, 1780; reprint, New York: Kelley, 1970), p. 214, defines a pirogue as "a sort of large canoe used in the Leeward Islands, South America and the Gulf of Mexico . . . composed of the trunks of two trees, hollowed and united into one fabric."

22. Antonio kept his word only "after a fashion" because the following day would have been 23 February. He did not return until 24 February.

23. It is incredible that Viaud should write thus of equality and feelings of kinship about a group which included a man he would subsequently kill and devour. This section is probably an editorial addition.

24. This is a mystifying argument, since elsewhere Viaud recorded that the various islands they visited were a mere six miles from the mainland. In clear weather it would have been visible.

25. Considerations of morality and humanity have no place in Viaud's pragmatic argument against murder at this time. They make his subsequent conversion to the necessity of murder more credible.

26. Here is an early indication that Viaud considered his slave expendable. Point man was the most dangerous position. A tall strong man who could best cope with unexpected hazards like undertow or potholes would have been the natural choice, yet Viaud appointed the smallest male in the group.

27. Barberry (*Berberis vulgaris*) is a shrub native to Europe and North America and common in what is now the southeastern United States with spiny shoots and pendulous racemes of small yellow flowers, succeeded by red, oblong, sharply acid berries. It is used mainly as a garnish for sauces and conserve. Eating sorrels would not be strange for Frenchmen. They were used extensively in French cooking and sometimes as medicine. For information on the subject I am grateful to Curt M. Peterson, professor of botany and microbiology, Auburn University.

28. Contrast this condescending comment with Viaud's earlier protestations that she was never a hindrance or an embarrassment (p. 61). Though right about her son, he was quite wrong about the lady. In the long run Madame La Couture would be able to go on when Viaud had reached the end of his tether.

29. Spanish moss (*Tillandsia usneioides*) grows in tropical Latin America and the southeastern United States and is very common on the Gulf of Mexico. Viaud actually called it *barbe espagnole* ("Spanish beard").

30. Perhaps what is now Goose Island, north of St. George Island.

31. This is perhaps the most repellent of the passages in which Viaud attempted to dehumanize his servant, the better for the reader to accept Viaud's subsequent monstrous behavior toward him. Viaud's usual technique in portraying the servant as less than human was to ignore him. He is never cited as having emotions or opinions, and we never even learn his name.

32. It defies belief that this obvious recourse had not been discussed previously by the castaways. It was the first expe-

dient they thought of when *Le Tigre* initially ran aground (p. 45).

33. This offensively sexist phrase would have been unexceptionable in the 1760s. Viaud intended a compliment.

34. Shrouds extend from a masthead to the sides of a vessel and hold up the mast. Braces are ropes to haul a sail into a required position and are usually (but probably not in this case) attached to the end of a yardarm. Sheets are ropes attached to the lower corners of a sail.

35. Although their physical weakness may have dissuaded the castaways from adding rollers to their first raft to remove it from the danger of destruction by high winds and tides, it seems incredibly feckless of them, after their first raft was destroyed, not to have resorted to rollers for launching the second. This episode is probably fictional.

36. The word here translated as "overcoat" is *redingote,* a long double-breasted garment providing protection for the chest, unlike the *habit,* the jacket Viaud wore underneath it, which would have been longer than its twentieth-century equivalent and, unlike its modern equivalent, could not be buttoned in front. The *veste,* the waistcoat worn beneath the *habit,* would have been sleeveless. Wearing so many layers of clothing in addition to a shirt was reasonable in the Floridian winter, but by mid-April sharing his clothes with young La Couture would have been no great sacrifice.

37. Unless this episode is purely fictional, it seems inconceivable that Madame La Couture would have left her son without seeing him. It may be that she had no choice in the matter. Viaud, ever anxious to portray himself in a favorable light, insisted that she consent to departure without seeing the lad. The truth may be that Viaud had decided to leave, and that the reluctant mother was not helped but forcibly dragged to the raft by Viaud and his servant.

38. As discussed in the introduction, animals other than the African and Asian beasts of the name (*Felis tigris* and

Felis leo) were commonly referred to as tigers and lions in eighteenth-century North America. The panther was then called a "tyger"; the jaguar was known as the American tiger and the puma as the American lion. It is conceivable that Viaud saw some of these but more probable that, frightened and in the fitful light of his fires, he misidentified less dangerous animals, which might well have uttered alarming sounds but certainly not the "dreadful roars" (Fr. *hurlements affreux*) mentioned on p. 83. All mention of tigers was omitted from the later French editions of *Naufrage*. Instead the author (or the editor) substituted: "In our terror, which increased constantly, we thought we saw among the beasts surrounding us animals of the most ferocious species, even some which are foreign to these regions. For a while fear blunted our faculties."

39. As told to George Swettenham soon after his rescue, Viaud's description differs in minor but horrible details from those given here. He told Swettenham that, after tying the black's hands, he blindfolded him with a handkerchief and sharpened his knife before cutting the poor fellow's throat (Swettenham to James Grant, 14 May 1766, Grant Papers, Bundle 243).

40. The head would seem the least likely part of a corpse to be cooked by a starving cannibal. This gruesome detail was probably invented by Dubois-Fontanelle.

41. I have translated the word *procurer* here as "preserve" because I suspect that the printer misread and set in type *procurer* for Viaud's intended *preserver*. *Procurer* ("to obtain") makes little sense. On the only occasion that fire was used by Viaud to obtain food (when snakes were overcome by smoke), it was unintentional, whereas he more than once used fire to preserve meat.

42. No river matching Viaud's description exists in this area today. However, on Bernard Romans's "Map of Part of East Florida" of 1772, which may be found at the end of P. Lee Phillips, *Notes on the Life and Works of Bernard Romans* (Gainesville: University of Florida Press, 1975), there

is a significant river on the Florida mainland north-northeast of Dog Island which would have necessitated travel upstream to cross. Its location roughly approximates that of New River.

43. In the first three-quarters of his narrative there is no mention of even a possible sexual relationship between Viaud and Madame La Couture. Toward the end of *Naufrage* Viaud touches on the possibility merely to reject it. Nevertheless there are hints, probably titillating to some eighteenth-century readers, that as they journeyed together, their behavior included a freedom which would have been quite improper in society of the day. When he returned to look for their flint, Viaud examined the makeshift bed on which both by clear implication had slept the previous night. Soon afterward he mentioned that for tinder he habitually used strips torn indiscriminately from his own and Madame La Couture's garments. Finally, the readiness with which both stripped to cross the river implied that barriers of modesty had quite disappeared. In the wretched physical state which Viaud and La Couture were in, disregarding convention did not necessarily imply dalliance.

44. In fact, as Viaud explained a few lines farther on, they lost their masks, leggings, moccasins, and gloves because immersion had ruined them.

45. Elizabeth Griffith translated the two foregoing sentences thus: "If my hopes should deceive me, it will not then be too late to expose myself, helpless and alone in this vast desert, accompanied only by my fears and dreading, every moment, that offended Heaven might let loose the savage beasts to devour me, as a just punishment for having forsaken you, while there remained the least possibility of affording you any manner of relief." Her translation is accurate but illogical. I suspect an omission by the eighteenth-century French typesetter and have added a clause ("If I abandoned you") which I think has the passage make more sense.

46. James Wright first appeared in the British Army List for 1764 (London: J. Millan, 1765) as an ensign in the Ninth Infantry Regiment, having been commissioned on 23 March 1764. He stayed with the Ninth and returned to America, losing his life at the Battle of Bennington in 1777 (Roger Lamb, *Memoir of his own Life* [Dublin: Jones, 1811], p. 85).

47. The Seven Years' War, 1756–63. I have found no record of Viaud's imprisonment.

48. George Yort Swettenham was an Irishman from Londonderry. During the Seven Years' War he was commissioned as an ensign in the 17th Infantry, but was seconded in 1760 to one of the South Carolina independent companies, which he joined as a lieutenant. He arrived in Charleston on 28 June and two days later set out to join Colonel Archibald Montgomery's expedition against the Cherokees (*South Carolina Gazette*, 5 July 1760). The failure of this expedition resulted in the dispatch of 1,200 British regulars to South Carolina for a punitive expedition in 1761. Its commander was Lieutenant Colonel James Grant. It was probably then that Swettenham made the acquaintance of this Scot, to whom he subsequently wrote a number of letters, including one about Viaud. Swettenham went with his independent company to Georgia, where he ran foul of the law, apparently for assaulting a trader (Kenneth Coleman and Milton Ready, eds., *Colonial Records of the State of Georgia* [Athens, Ga.: University of Georgia Press, 1976], vol. 28, pt. 1:391–92). With the end of the Seven Years' War in 1763, Swettenham was retired on half pay but in 1764, perhaps through Grant's patronage, was appointed a lieutenant in the Ninth Regiment (*Georgia Gazette*, 1 November 1764). He was sent briefly from St. Augustine to the small garrison at St. Mark's, Apalache, which he commanded from 12 December 1765 until 2 October 1766 (Mark F. Boyd, "From a Remote Frontier, Part 1, San Marcos de Apalache, 1763–1769," *Florida Historical Quarterly* 19 [1941]: 187). He returned to his native Ireland in the packet *Hillsborough* in

1767 (George C. Rogers, Jr., and David R. Chesnutt, eds., *The Papers of Henry Laurens* [Columbia, S.C.:University of South Carolina Press, 1976] 5: 219n). Swettenham was promoted to captain on 2 March 1776, on the outbreak of the American Revolution, and returned to America in 1777. His last appearance in the British Army list was in 1784, still as a captain.

49. A few days later Swettenham wrote that "We have the greatest reason to think that the dead body found on the beach was the woman's husband," rather than Desclau, but explained no further (Swettenham to Grant, 14 May 1766, Grant Papers, Bundle 243).

50. Elizabeth Griffith translated the word *outarde* as "bustard," which is exclusively an Old World bird. But *outarde* also means the blackhead Canada goose which abounded on the Gulf Coast at the time of Viaud's ordeal (Romans, *Concise Natural History*, p. 302).

51. It is uncertain from what part of St. George Island Viaud and Madame La Couture crossed to the mainland, if indeed they ever did, but to get to St. Mark's, if they had stayed close to the coast they would potentially have had to negotiate what are now called New River, Crooked River, Ochlockonee River, Sopchoppy River, Postum Bayou, Purify Creek, Old Creek, Spring Creek, Gordon Creek, Graves Creek, East Goose Creek, Flat Creek, Big West Creek and the Wakulla River. If they were no larger then than they are today, crossing them would have posed little problem.

52. There was no surgeon at St. Mark's, but there was a surgeon's mate named Dyerson (Swettenham to Gage, 13 January 1766, in Mark F. Boyd, "From a Remote Frontier, Part 2," *Florida Historical Quarterly*, 20 [1941–42]: 382).

53. Viaud's symptoms, including weakness in the leg muscles and swelling produced by fluid collection in various parts of the body, suggest that he may have suffered from wet beri-beri, a very dangerous condition often accompanied by heart failure. It is caused by a deficiency of thia-

mine, or Vitamin B^2, which may be found in cereals, peas, beans, and other vegetables. During his ordeal Viaud had of course eaten none of these foods.

54. Viaud seems to have had no conception that his practice of cannibalism might have earned him contempt, but his opinion of the captain was not unique. Swettenham described him as a "brute" who, for his own profit, had sold provisions intended for his crew and passengers (Swettenham to Grant, 14 May 1766, Grant Papers, Bundle 243).

55. James Grant (1720–1806) studied law before in 1764 receiving a captain's commission in the Royal Scots, with whom he fought at Fontenoy and Culloden. In 1757 he was promoted to major and served in America and was briefly a prisoner of war. After promotion to lieutenant colonel in 1760, he was appointed to lead a punitive expedition against the Cherokees in 1761 and subsequently became governor of East Florida in 1763. He assumed his governorship in 1764 and remained at St. Augustine until 1771. He took command of a regiment in Ireland in 1772 and entered Parliament in 1773. After the American Revolution broke out, he returned to America and fought at Long Island in 1776 as a brigadier general. He fought at Brandywine in 1777 and as a major general at Monmouth Courthouse, where his conduct provoked the criticism of superiors. He redeemed himself by capturing and holding the French island of St. Lucia in 1778. Grant returned to Britain in 1779, where he engaged in parliamentary and (as a full general) military activities, until his death in 1806. See Mark M. Boatner III, *Encyclopaedia of the American Revolution* (New York: McKay, 1975), pp. 442–44.

56. St. Augustine was a small garrison town overlooking, on its southern side, the embouchure of the St. Sebastien River. On the northern, eastern, and western sides were fortifications surrounding four streets that ran from north to south and eleven streets that ran at right angles to them. "The castle" is the Castillo de San Marcos, a fort in the northeast corner dominating St. Augustine's small har-

bor. (Public Record Office, CO 700 Florida 23). There were perhaps 350 buildings of all sorts in the town. The governor's house and gardens were large, bounded on the north by fortifications, and gave onto the town square to the south (PRO, CO 700 Florida 8).

57. With his phrase "chez M. Grant" Viaud gave the impression that he was a guest in the governor's apartments in the fort. So he may have been for part of the thirty-eight days (13 June–21 July) that he was in St. Augustine, but Grant's contingent account reveals that for twenty-one of these days he boarded with a Mrs. Margaret McPhail (PRO, CO 5/548:397).

58. A snow was a large two-masted vessel. The mainmast was conventionally rigged with a square sail but the smaller mast behind it bore a triangular trysail.

Appendix 1

Extract from George Swettenham to James Grant, 14 May 1766, Grant Papers, Ballindalloch Castle, Banffshire, Scotland

. . . [Ensign James Wright] went off in a small canoe to investigate [the reported discovery of a corpse washed up on a beach] but the weather was so bad that he was obliged to return without discovering anything. In a few days after he went in a larger, and on an island about thirty or forty miles from hence and six miles distant from the shore, he found a Frenchman and woman in the most miserable situation; they had been there two months and eight days, were left by an Indian who had promised to conduct them to St. Marks, but who robbed them of all they saved from the shipwreck; they were obliged to kill a Negro for their subsistance [sic], the story of which is shocking—his tying his hands, his handkerchief over his eye, his sharping [sic] his knife and then cutting his throat—is terrible. A few scraps of this miserable wretch was their provision when Mr. Wright took them up. On another island, a few miles distant, they found a French lad about sixteen years of age, son to the woman, so reduced that he could scarcely speak and was obliged to be carried on board of the boat: he could not have lived [another] twelve hours.

Appendix 2

Extract from James Grant to the Board of Trade, 5 August 1766, CO5/548:199–200, Great Britain, Public Record Office, Kew

. . . [Indian] hunters have lately fallen in with a party of poor unhappy Frenchmen, who were cast away upon this coast and they most barbarously murdered some of them to get plunder; the headman, upon hearing this, took alarm, being afraid that some of the king's [i.e., George III] subjects had been killed; they met together and were determined to give satisfaction by putting the guilty Indians to death, but finding upon enquiry that there were no white men killed (so they call the English), they thought there was no great harm done. But that no doubt might remain of their good intentions, Talachea, the great man of the nation, sent a messenger five hundred miles to explain the matter to me, and lest an accident should happen to the messenger, he sent a talk to the same purpose to the officer at St. Mark's to be forwarded to me. They pretend that the French killed two women and a boy of their people who they found in the woods, but to that I don't give much credit and I have told them that the Great King [George III] is at peace with the French and the Spaniards, and that he will be very angry with his children if they kill any of them. I send your lordship the account which I received from one of the Frenchmen who escaped with the captain's wife and son; he came from St. Mark's in a miserable condition.